The First
Five Years

The First Five Years

From birth to primary school, understand and encourage your child's development

Dr Philippa Kaye

white
LADDER

First edition published in Great Britain in 2015 by White
Ladder Press, an imprint of Crimson Publishing Ltd
This reprint first published in Great
Britain in 2021 by White Ladder
An imprint of Hodder & Stoughton
An Hachette UK company

1

A CIP catalogue record for this title is
available from the British Library

Paperback ISBN 978 191033 607 6

Typeset by IDS UK (DataConnections) Ltd
Printed and bound in Great Britain by
Clays Ltd, Elcograf S.p.A.

Hodder & Stoughton policy is to use papers that are
natural, renewable and recyclable products and made
from wood grown in sustainable forests. The logging and
manufacturing processes are expected to conform to the
environmental regulations of the country of origin.

Hodder & Stoughton Ltd
Carmelite House
50 Victoria Embankment
London EC4Y 0DZ

www.hodder.co.uk

To my children, Harrison, Edward & Madeline; watching you grow and develop has been, and continues to be, simply fascinating.

Contents

Contents

About the author

Dr Philippa Kaye MB, BS Hons, MA (Cantab), nMRCGP, DCH, DRCOG, DFSRH works as a GP in London and has established herself as a highly motivated and dedicated young doctor. She is the author of *Child Health Essentials* (Dorling Kindersley 2011), *Your Pregnancy Week by Week* (Vermilion 2010), *Childhood & Adolescent Diabetes* (Sheldon Press 2008) and *The Fertility Handbook* (Sheldon Press 2007). She has also been a contributor to *Pregnancy Day by Day* (Dorling Kindersley 2009).

Aside from being a young, working mother of three children, she has appeared on BBC radio, various podcasts and has been the resident medical expert for leading parenting magazine, *Junior*. In addition to this, she has contributed regularly to other magazines such as *Prima Mother and Baby*, *Bliss*, *Junior Pregnancy and Baby*, *Reveal* and *Sugar*.

Acknowledgements

There are always many people involved in the creation of a book, from my supportive agent, Jane, of Graham Maw Christie literacy agency, to my editor, Hugh Brune, at Crimson and his whole team. I also have to mention all the many, many children and their families whom I have watched grow as part of my job as a GP, who have all taught me as much as any book on child development ever could! Being a governor at my son's local primary school has given me a new insight into child development, adding an educational and social perspective as well as the medical, so thanks are given to the governing body, staff and children. Thanks also to Victoria Hayward, child and adolescent psychotherapist-in-training, for many stimulating discussions regarding child development and relationships, and in particular about the theories of the paediatrician Donald Winnicott.

Finally, as ever, thanks must be given to my (ever growing) family! I have always been surrounded by babies and children, even as a child myself, and this experience and insight continues to be invaluable, as is their continuing and unwavering support.

Introduction

The First Five Years aims to give you an understanding of your child's development from birth to 5 years old. These are the years in which your child goes from being a newborn, totally dependent on you for every need, to an increasingly independent young child heading off to school. The changes involved in this process are huge and your child's brain and nervous system will be growing and developing faster now than at any other stage in life: by the end of the first year, the brain will have tripled in size!

Every parent is concerned whether or not their child is developing at the expected rate, and often parents compare with their other children or friend's children. However, different children will develop and achieve milestones at different ages, just as one child may lose his first tooth earlier than another. This book aims to give you guidance about what can be expected at each age group as well as giving you, hopefully enjoyable, tips about how to stimulate and encourage your child's development through playing.

Child development is divided into the following areas.

- Gross motor development: called 'mobility' within this book. This covers use of the large muscles of the body, in the core and the limbs. In practical terms this means when your baby will hold his head up, sit up, crawl, walk and then run, jump, hop, climb stairs and ride a tricycle, among other skills.
- Fine motor development: here called 'handling skills'. This is the ability to use the small muscles of the fingers and hands to handle objects. Starting from when your baby finds his hands and uses his whole hand to grasp an object, to your child being able to have enough control to handle a pencil and write, cut with scissors and build with blocks, for example.
- Speech and language development: this encompasses both 'receptive' and 'expressive' language, which respectively mean your child's ability to understand others and then to communicate in return. Aspects covered in this book include understanding tone of voice, the appearance of first words, the linking together of words to form sentences and the ability to retell a story.

- Social and emotional development: this covers the areas of eating (which is a social activity!), dressing and toileting as well as interacting with other people. Starting from eye contact and the first smile, continuing to your child feeding himself, and then to making friends.
- Cognitive development: termed 'problem solving' within the book as this area covers your child's ability to learn, explore and solve problems. From learning that objects exist even if they cannot be seen, to working out how to play with toys, complete puzzles and learn new skills.

All of these areas of development are dependent on hearing and vision – the ability to see and hear. In order for your child to learn to speak, he needs to first be able to hear the sounds required to make words, and then to hear his own voice as he begins to make noises. The ability to pick up a toy depends on being able to see the toy. Your child's hearing will be assessed within a few days of birth and you will be asked questions, such as whether or not your baby looks at your face, at his six week check. Any potential problems need to be picked up as early as possible so that relevant treatment can be offered. If you have any concerns about your child's vision or hearing, see your doctor.

Your child learns though play, discovering the world through play, which is essential for his development. As the famous paediatrician and psychoanalyst said:

> 66 Play provides an organisation for initiation of emotional relationships, and so enables social contacts to develop 99
> **Winnicott, 1942, Why Children Play**

When scribbling on a piece of paper and babbling to you about what he is doing, your child is not merely scribbling or playing, but having the motor skills required to sit up, hold a crayon and make marks, which may have meaning for him, and he is talking to you and interacting with you at the same time!

How to use this book

This book is divided into chapters covering various age brackets between birth and 5 years old. Within each chapter an area of child development, as listed above, is described along with tips and games to encourage your child's development. There is some overlap between the chapters, for example 3–6 months and 6–9 months, because child development is not exact: not every child will achieve a skill at the same time, so your child may be crawling earlier than another baby. Significant changes in vision and hearing are also covered, for example from black and white vision to colour vision. There are also chapters discussing common situations and how to play at each age in order to encourage particular developmental skills, for example at the supermarket or household chores play.

As a parent myself, I know that sometimes your child's behaviour can be challenging! However, having an understanding of why he is reacting in a particular way, be it throwing a tantrum, not being able to share, or even asking incessant 'why' questions, can help you to find a method to deal with the behaviour. This needs to be a method with which you are both comfortable and a method that your child understands. Having insight into the cause of the behaviour can help to give you tools to deal with it. As such, there is a chapter covering common issues such as separation anxiety, tantrums and head banging.

Before you know it, time has flown by and your tiny newborn has grown into an increasingly independent toddler and then a young child, heading off to school. The final chapter of the book covers settling into the first year of formal schooling (Reception), how to help your child with this process and how to support learning.

Is my child developing as expected?

For many parents, there is a lot of anxiety about how their child is developing. Is he developing at the right speed? Does it matter if a sibling or a friend stood up/spoke earlier than him? Many parents come to my surgery with questions about their child's development, wanting to know if they should be concerned. This book aims to alleviate some of these worries, describing the average ages at which a child develops various skills. Children will develop at different rates, most of which are within the range of appropriate development. Some children will stand up and walk at 1 year old, others not until 17 months old, neither of which would be a concern. Where appropriate, age limits or red flag signs are given for when you may need to see your doctor, for example if your child is not walking at 18 months old. However, even here there may not be a problem, for example bottom shufflers often walk a bit later. If you are concerned about your child's development at any point, then see your health visitor or doctor. Postnatal depression is not covered within this book, but if you are feeling low, or not bonding with your baby, or simply not coping, then do seek help from your doctor.

Boys and girls

A common discussion amongst parents is whether boys and girls develop at different speeds. It is true that boys and girls have physically different brains and are exposed to different hormonal levels, with boys being exposed to more testosterone. It is also true that a baby's brain develops extremely rapidly, and that particular areas of the brain may develop at different speeds in boys and girls. For example, the language and emotion areas in girls may develop faster, and this *may* mean that girls are more likely to talk earlier. However, this might just as likely be shaped by environment and genes. Do some girls talk and express emotions earlier than boys because girls' brains are wired to do so, or because we give them more encouragement? Similarly, when a child is upset, do we as parents tend to treat a crying boy differently from a crying girl, and so encourage different behaviours in boys and girls?

Generally speaking, there is little difference between the early development of girls and boys, and so all the advice that follows applies equally to both sexes. It is the plasticity of a young child's brain that makes it so remarkable. If an area of the brain is used, it will develop, so encouraging your child to have a wide range of interests and being in tune with emotions will aid development. And although you may notice that your son walked at 13 months old and your daughter at 16 months old, this is not a significant difference as both are within the expected age of walking (which is between 12 and 18 months old).

NB: Throughout the book, to keep things simple, I have referred to children consistently as 'he'. However, to be clear, as noted above, all the stages apply equally to girls and boys.

I know from my own experience as a parent and a doctor that having a baby (who grows into a young child) is an overwhelming experience, full of joy and wonder, as well as a good dollop of terror! This book aims to guide you, not through the practicalities of weaning or potty training, but rather to help you see the changes in your child's development and how to encourage this development through play. In our busy lives it can be hard to take the time to allow your child to walk on every wall, jump between the paving stones or pick up every fallen leaf, but these are not time wasting: rather, they are an opportunity to learn and develop through the everyday activities of life. Of course, not every time that you sort the laundry can involve your child trying to match the socks, but taking the time occasionally can be both educational and, more importantly, fun for you both! This book is not meant to be prescriptive in any way: much of what is described in the book may be instinctive. Not all play has to have an underlying lesson. Rather, the book aims to show you the value within all play, even if it seems like you are mucking about pretending to be a lion!

Part 1

0–3 months

Mobility

Although your baby is not going anywhere without being carried at the moment, his gross motor system is still developing. He currently has a reflex – an automatic movement or reaction (such as when a doctor taps your knee and your leg jumps) – called the 'Moro' or 'startle' reflex. This reflex is triggered by a sudden loud noise, or by a sudden loss of head or neck support when being held. The reflex causes your baby to throw his head back and extend and throw out his arms and legs, quickly followed by him pulling his arms and legs back in, like he is trying to cuddle himself. The purpose of this reflex is not clear but it is thought that it may help him to cling on when being carried. Even the sound of his own cry can startle your baby into this reflex! He will probably lose this reflex by about 3 months old. Various reflexes are present at birth, which will be described in this book. Some of them, such as the startle reflex described above, are present for a certain period of time before disappearing, while others, such as the blinking reflex (when you automatically blink if something touches your eye), persist throughout adulthood.

Initially you will find that your baby cannot hold his head up at all: when you carry him upright against your shoulder he will lay his head on your shoulder, but this does not last long and soon you will find that he begins to hold his head up on your shoulder. If you lay him on his front, by 6 weeks old he will be able to turn his face to the side, followed by his raising his head up for short periods of time. By

3 months old he will be able to raise his head for longer periods of time and may even be able to hold himself up on his elbows and forearms (see Figure 1). If you pull him up by his hands from lying on his back to a sitting position, at 6 weeks old he will not be able to support his head at all, and by 3 months old he will still need help but will have more head control. When lying on his back he will start to kick both legs and may even be able to roll from his back to his side and back again, but not roll over.

Other reflexes present at birth include the placing reflex: if your baby is held upright and the top of his foot gently stroked, for example by the edge of a table or chair, he will pick up his foot and place it on top of the surface. This reflex is lost at approximately 6 to 8 weeks old. At the same time he will lose another reflex, called the stepping reflex: if your baby is held upright and his foot placed firmly against a surface, such as a table, he will appear to take steps.

Figure 1

> ### How to help
> - Allow him time free from being swaddled/wrapped in blankets or restrictive clothing so that he can learn to kick his legs.
> - Introduce tummy time, which helps him to strengthen the muscles in his neck. You can do this from birth (but do not leave your baby to sleep on his tummy).

Handling skills

As yet your baby does not even realise that he has hands, never mind being able to control them. However, in the first 3 months he will start to make jerky arm movements as he learns to control his arms. You may notice that your newborn baby generally has his fingers clenched into a fist, but by 3 months old his hands become more open. He has some reflexes involving his hands: the 'palmar grasp' reflex occurs when the palm of his hand is stimulated by putting something in it, and his fingers curl around the object. So if you tickle or gently stroke your baby's palm with your finger he will grab your finger and hold on tight! This reflex will be lost at approximately 3 to 4 months old. It is thought that this reflex may help with voluntary grasping of objects later on. If you put a rattle in his hand he may be able to hold on to it momentarily.

> ### How to help
> - Encourage him to hold your finger. While it may be a reflex, it is still fun and can help with bonding. Allowing him to hold on to toys such as a rattle may help him to learn about objects and about arm movements.

Speech and language

Although your baby does not have language at this point he will quickly learn to communicate with you without words. He will start to coo or gurgle and may well be delighted by the sound of his own voice.

He may gurgle or coo as a response to your voice. He will be startled by a loud noise and will recognise your voice; if he is whimpering he may well quieten down at the reassuring sound of your voice. Let him watch your face and pick up on the non-verbal cues in your expression – there may not be words yet but you are still communicating!

Your baby's cry is the way in which he is communicating with you. Even in the first few weeks he will develop different cries to mean different things such as hunger, wetness or discomfort, or loneliness. You will quickly learn to distinguish his cries, often to the amazement of other people! He will often stop crying when he is picked up, showing that he understands that you have come to meet his needs.

How to help

- Spend time looking at each other, talk to him even though he cannot yet answer back, and sing to him. He will love the sound of your voice, whether or not it is in tune, and will find it comforting.
- Respond to his crying, which helps him to realise that crying serves a purpose and that you will respond to him, making him feel safe and secure.

Social and emotional development

At this young age your baby will be breast- or bottle-fed and has various reflexes to help him to do so. The 'rooting' reflex occurs when you stroke or touch his cheek: doing this makes him turn towards the side you stroked, with his mouth open looking for food. Your baby may trigger the reflex himself if he accidentally touches his own face. This reflex generally disappears by the time he is 3 or 4 months old, when your baby will voluntarily turn his head for food as he will understand what the breast or bottle means to him. Another feeding reflex is the 'sucking' reflex: this is when something (a nipple or bottle teat) is placed in your baby's mouth and he automatically starts to suck. This reflex is lost at approximately 3 to 4 months old, when he begins to suck voluntarily as opposed to automatically. The sucking reflex has two parts: the first is as the nipple is drawn into the mouth when your baby automatically presses or squeezes the nipple between his tongue and palate; the second is when he then sucks with a milking action using his tongue to express the milk down from the areola or base of the nipple. These reflexes help with breastfeeding: if you stimulate your baby's cheek with your hand or breast he will turn towards your breast with an open mouth rooting for the nipple, and once his mouth is wide open you can put your nipple in his mouth and he will automatically begin sucking to get milk. These reflexes are necessary for survival: your baby is born with an innate ability to look for food.

Perhaps the first obvious developmental milestone is that of your baby smiling, a truly magical moment which you will probably spend a lot of time trying to recreate over and over! The first smiles tend to appear at approximately 6 to 8 weeks old. Initially this smile is your baby's response to something he feels, hears, smells or sees; however, this communication quickly develops as he realises that when he smiles, you smile in return. This is quickly followed by a responsive smile: you smile at him (in a big obvious way) and he then smiles in return. By 3 months old he will be smiling in anticipation, when he sees you or if he is excited about a familiar routine such as feeding or bath time.

Your baby will love looking at your face, and will often look extremely intently at your face or even at objects arranged to look like a face! This is the beginning of him being able to read the non-verbal communication that is your facial expression. By 6 weeks old he will be able to fix on your face and follow you with his eyes as you move around. Your newborn learns to recognise you, his mother, very quickly; your voice, your face, perhaps even your smell, but as yet he does not understand what 'mother' means. This will come later, but for now he recognises you as the person that is most familiar and the provider of food, comfort and cuddles.

The world is a very different place to the environment within the womb, and so your baby is easily overwhelmed. In the womb everything was muffled, including light and sounds, so the bright lights and loud noises of the outside world can be too stimulating and overwhelming. Your baby may then need to be soothed with quiet words, sounds or white noise (a continuous noise such as radio static, which he may find calming).

How to help

- Hold and cuddle him – lots and lots! This helps him feel safe and comforted and also helps with the bonding process. Cuddling is mutually beneficial: it makes both of you feel good! He loves physical contact, being held, cuddled, rocked and stroked and the stimulation of touch. He may also enjoy baby massage, which helps him learn about his body and is often a great way to calm or comfort him.
- Hold him about 30cm away from your face. This is the distance at which he can focus (approximately the distance from you holding him in your arms to your face). When he is quiet watch him focus on your face and show him what to do: by smiling in an obvious way, you may well be rewarded with a smile in return!

Problem solving

Initially your baby is a swirling whirl of feelings that he may not comprehend. For example, he does not understand that you and he are separate beings; currently he thinks you are there to know and meet his needs. At first he does not understand what is happening in the world outside him, that he has parents, that someone helps him when he is crying. He knows that he feels content and full, or perhaps just not uncomfortable or not hungry, after feeding but he does not know that he needs to feed to take away the sensation of hunger, or that being full makes him feel content or happy. He cries due to a feeling he has inside that he generally does not understand, be it hunger or a need for comfort, and as yet he does not realise that he feels better because you feed or cuddle him. He also does not yet have a concept of time, so every emotion feels like an emergency which he wants dealt with straightaway!

Although he is a little ball of feelings, your baby does not yet have thoughts associated with those feelings. He can confuse your feelings with his own: it is difficult to hide how you are feeling from your baby, so if you are upset or anxious he will pick up on this but not yet understand that these are your feelings and not necessarily his, as he does not yet know that you are two separate beings with separate feelings. This means that if you are upset, he may also feel upset or anxious and respond accordingly, at this age often by crying or niggling. So when you are feeling anxious, tearful or even just exhausted and frazzled your baby may pick up on this and therefore become more difficult to comfort. The calmer you are, the calmer your baby may be.

Hearing and vision

Your baby could hear even while in the womb and you may notice that he recognises your voice, perhaps quietening or stilling when he hears you even from birth. He may also startle or cry at very loud or sudden sounds. Your baby will have a hearing check within a few days or weeks of birth. Within the first 3 months he will start to turn towards the sound of your voice.

At birth your baby can see in black and white and shades of grey and focuses best on objects approximately 20–30cm away from his face, which is about the distance, when being held at the breast, to his mother's face. Even at this early stage, he seems to prefer looking at faces (or pictures of faces), though you may notice that he does not appear to fix or focus well – this takes practice, but he does enjoy looking at black and white contrasting pictures. Your face will be the first object that he begins to recognise as familiar.

Within a week or so of birth his eyes and brain have developed further and your baby will now be able to see some colour, specifically bright primary colours. Initially, you may notice that his eyes do not always move together, but that one eye may drift in a squint. In a very young baby this is normal as he learns to control his eye muscles. However, if a squint is still present at his postnatal check (generally 6 to 8 weeks after birth), then tell your doctor, who will be able to refer you to an eye specialist. By the second and third month, your baby's focus will improve and you will notice that he fixes his eyes on you (or an object) and follows you with his eyes as you move around. He will also turn towards a light source.

Should I worry? Is my child developing correctly?

See your doctor when your baby is 3 months old if:

- he does not suck or feed well
- he has a persistent squint
- he does not smile
- he does not startle to a loud noise
- he does not look at you or follow your face
- his hands are in a permanent fist which does not open
- he is very floppy or very stiff.

You should also see your doctor if you feel that you cannot cope with your baby, or if you feel that you cannot respond to him.

2

3–6 months

Mobility

If you lay your baby on his back, his legs are now strong enough for him to kick and straighten them. Previous to this you may have noticed that he may not have always straightened his legs out when lying down, instead lying in the fetal position with his legs and arms curled up and inwards into his body. Whilst lying on his back at around 4 months old he will become fascinated by his hands and later on by his feet. You will notice that he spends lots of time lifting his arms so that he can see his hands, waving them and moving them in front of his face. This is called 'hand regard' and is when he notices his hands for the first time. Hands are simply fascinating to him and looking at them is the first step to using them, working out where they are in space and how he can control them. As time progresses he will learn to reach for toys, initially this may be with what seems like wild uncontrolled movements. He may have worked out where his arms are but it takes a little longer to work out how to control them!

Your baby now has control of his head: he holds his head up when you hold him upright against your shoulder. At approximately 4 months old, if you pull him up by his hands from lying on his back to sitting, your baby will have control of his head, which will no longer lag behind. By 6 months old, he is able to anticipate this action and brace his neck with his shoulders.

When lying on his tummy, your baby is able to lift his head off the floor to a 45 degree angle and then lift his upper chest as well, aiming towards being able to support the weight of his head and chest on his hands (see Figure 2). He can also lie on his front and lift his head and both arms and legs off the floor at the same time to kick them while balancing on his tummy. As he gets older you may find that on his front he can move around in a circular motion by lifting his arms and legs and kicking. Allowing him time to kick and play on his tummy will help to strengthen the muscles in his core and limbs. You may see this when you hold him upright and he begins to bear some weight on his legs.

In a sitting position, your baby can hold his head up and steady but he will not be able to sit unaided. However, he can sit supported, for example in your arms, in the corner of a sofa or propped up with cushions (though if not supported enough, he will veer over to one

Figure 2

side). Initially your baby will sit with a rounded back but as he gets stronger, his back will straighten. He will also be able to sit upright holding your hands.

By 6 months old your baby has lost one of his early reflexes, called the 'asymmetrical tonic neck reflex' (ATNR). This is a reflex that occurs when your baby turns his head to one side. As he turns his neck to one side, let's say the left, the arm and leg on the left side will extend and stretch out towards the left (the side to which he is turning), and the arm and leg on the opposite side, the right side, will bend inwards. This is sometimes called the 'fencer's pose' as it looks like the baby is holding out his arm to hold a fencing foil (see Figure 3). The opposite happens when turning the head to the right side, with the right arm and leg extending out and the left arm and leg curling inwards.

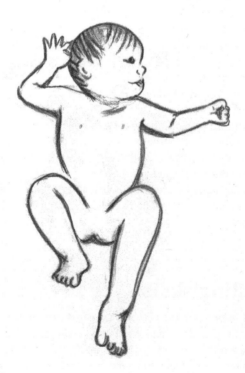

Figure 3

The ATNR reflex is developed in the womb and is thought to help with the rotation required during delivery. It also helps to develop muscle tone and is thought to be the start of hand–eye coordination. This reflex is generally lost by the time your baby is 6 months old – your baby cannot start rolling until this reflex is lost, as otherwise his arm is in the way, preventing him from turning over. Once this reflex is lost, your baby may start to roll over, initially from front to back and then from back to front. Losing the ATNR reflex also allows your baby to cross the midline, so that he can lift an arm or hand on one side and cross it over his middle to the other side, which helps him to grab toys. Initially you will find that at about 3 to 4 months old he swipes at toys and often misses. As time progresses he will become more accurate at grabbing toys.

> ## How to help
> - Allow him daily tummy time. This helps him to strengthen the muscles in his neck (to hold up his heavy head!) and to develop the strength in the muscles of his core. Initially, he may get frustrated and start crying after a few minutes because it is hard work to keep his head up, but this does not mean that he does not like tummy time. Give him time to play on his front, but if he gets distressed pick him up or turn him over and have another go later on.
> - Play with him lying on his back, allowing him space and time to kick his arms and legs.
> - Blow raspberries on his tummy! This helps him to enjoy lying down and you are rewarded with smiles, laughter and excited kicking.

Handling skills

Once your baby has found his hands and feet, he may spend a lot of time playing with them. This means not only feeling them, but also popping them (and any other object he finds) into his mouth. His lips and mouth are full of nerve endings which give him information about the object he is holding; what it feels like, its shape and texture. At 3 to 4 months old your baby will hold a toy such as a rattle if you put it in his hand. He will likely put it straight into his mouth to have a good feel of it. As he gets older and becomes more accurate at grabbing toys, he may give it a shake to see what it does first, and then put it in his mouth!

How to help

- Allow him to examine his toys and objects with his hands or mouth as long as the objects are not small enough for him to swallow and do not have parts that could come off and be swallowed or present a choking hazard.
- Start playing with, and showing him, rattles and other toys, perhaps holding them up so he can try to bat them or grab them.
- Put toys close to him so that he can touch them. At first this might be by mistake but once he finds the toy by accident he can then try to find it again.
- Use brightly coloured and interesting objects or rattles to grab his attention and rotate them so that he can play with different objects.
- Let him explore. Give him time to play with his toys and explore them with his mouth, allowing him space to concentrate on what he is doing.
- Change his environment, even by moving him around the room, so that he has different things to look at and explore.

Speech and language

The first form of communication that your baby has with you is crying. He cries and you pick him up and attend to his needs, be it a cuddle, a nappy change or a feed. You may think you have simply fed him but your baby is learning that if he cries you respond, so he is communicating with you. However, by this age, he will be making some noises which are not simply crying: he will make some cooing and gurgling sounds and then will start to make babbling noises. You may find that he starts babbling and then goes quiet as if he is listening for a response or even that you can start to have a conversation with him (you say something and he babbles and then waits for you to respond). He may also start talking to his toys, having conversations with them, and practising for speech. He will also turn his head towards a noise, looking for its source.

How to help

- Talk to him and allow him the time to talk back! This not only helps him to develop speech, but also to develop the understanding that you are separate from him. (Initially your baby does not realise that you are not simply part of him.) This is a difficult idea for him to grasp; that you are separate from him and that language and communication helps to bind you together and helps you to understand each other. Talking to your baby is the first step towards this.
- Repeat back any cooing noises or other sounds that he makes, and have a conversation of these noises. This helps him to learn the sound he has made and how to make it again.
- Speak clearly and let him see your mouth when you speak so that he begins to learn the shapes required of his lips and mouth to create speech. You may find that he starts to copy your faces.
- Name objects in simple language and show him what you are talking about – nappy, bottle, rattle – so that he begins to learn that objects have names.

Social and emotional development

Between 3 and 6 months old your baby is beginning to understand that he is out of the womb and in the world on his own. Although he may understand that you are the person who meets his needs, he still does not understand that the whole of life and everyone in it is not controlled by him, and that you and he are separate beings. This concept takes time: however, he is beginning to develop the idea that relationships are rewarding and beneficial to him. He becomes aware not only that you meet his physical needs by feeding and changing him, but also that you make him feel safe and nurtured. He sees you smiling at him, that he makes you happy, and this gives him an idea of his own self-worth and self-esteem, making the relationship mutually beneficial. His relationship with you is the first one that he has and is the basis for his relationships with others. To do this he will make lots of eye contact with you, you look at each other, and his eyes follow you and your face as you move across his field of vision.

He loves to look at faces, especially yours, and by spending time looking at your face and making eye contact with you, your baby will learn to understand the non-verbal cues that you give with your facial expression. He begins to understand that when you are smiling you are happy and he will often smile back. If you look upset or angry you may notice that your baby can also read this emotion from your expression and he may look anxious or distressed too. At this age your baby will be happy to smile at both you and strangers. He does not have an idea of stranger anxiety; smiling at you is enjoyable so he will smile at others. He will start to laugh and giggle out loud, squeal with joy and delight, kick his legs and wave his arms when he is excited and happy. As you speak to him he responds by smiling, laughing and kicking and will show you what he enjoys, such as bath time or being tickled.

Your baby will also lose a reflex called the 'tongue thrust' reflex between approximately 4 and 6 months old. This reflex means that if something touches the back of his tongue, he gags and pushes it out; so if you touch your baby's tongue with a spoon before this age he will push against you, pushing the spoon out of his mouth. This may be a protective reflex to stop him choking on objects. Other primitive reflexes such as the sucking and rooting reflexes (see Chapter 1) will be lost by 4 months old. The current recommendation is to start weaning at 6 months old, by which point these reflexes will be lost.

How to help
- Give him an unbreakable play mirror at eye level, perhaps during tummy time, or put a mirror low on the wall so that he can see himself. Your baby will not yet understand that he is looking at his own reflection but will enjoy looking at, and interacting with, his own face!

Problem solving

Your baby will be learning through exploring objects and his surroundings, by feeling, by putting things in his mouth and by playing with things to see what they do. He is beginning to have an understanding of his relationship with you and about communicating with you. He starts to understand his routine: for example, he might get excited when he sees his bottle, or when you take his clothes off for bath time, proving that his memory is developing and he understands what is about to happen. He will respond to noises and show that he enjoys music; he smiles at the sound of your voice, showing that he recognises you and your importance to him.

How to help
- Try playing some music and watch him respond by kicking his legs.
- Introduce toys that make different noises, for example by shaking them or banging them. This teaches him that his actions have consequences – when I hit this, it makes a sound.
- Show him clearly what you are doing and talk through your daily routine, such as preparing for bath time. When you take off all his clothes and lay him on the mat, with the sound of the bath running, he will understand that he is about to have a bath.

Hearing and vision

By 6 months old your baby will respond to sounds, perhaps by gurgling, and will become excited or happy to see you. As his hearing develops you will notice that he responds even to quiet sounds, if he is concentrating and not distracted by play!

During this time your baby's visual acuity continues to improve and he will be looking at, and then reaching for, objects. His colour vision will also continue to develop, allowing him to see the full range of colours.

Should I worry? Is my child developing correctly?

See your doctor when your baby is 6 months old if:

- he cannot hold up his head
- he is very floppy and does not try to kick his legs
- he does not follow your face with his eyes
- he cannot sit with support
- he has a persistent squint
- he does not smile
- he is not making any sounds at all.

You should also see your doctor if you feel that you are not coping at home.

6–9 months

Mobility

Rollin', rollin', rollin' – between 6 and 9 months old your baby will grow from a baby who lies on the floor happily looking around to one who can sit on his own and can start to move, generally by rolling, though he may even start to crawl.

When on the floor on his tummy you may notice that your baby lifts his head and chest off the mat, sometimes looking like he is about to do push-ups! He may then start to move along the floor on his tummy in a 'commando crawl'. As his neck and arm muscles become stronger he will learn to roll over; generally this is from front to back first and then from back to front, though it does not matter which way around. After rolling from his front to his back, he may get 'stuck' when he cannot get back again! On his front your baby may then begin to push himself up onto his knees and practise rocking as a precursor to crawling. He will probably start to crawl between 7 and 10 months old (see Chapter 4).

Your baby will be able to sit supported, propped up in the corner of the sofa or with lots of pillows around him. He will then learn to sit unsupported, initially for a few minutes at a time, and often with his legs stuck out in front of him like two sides of a triangle to help with balance. As the muscles in his core (his abdomen and back) get stronger, he will be able to sit alone. A baby at this age generally sits with a straight back when sitting unsupported.

Fascinated by his feet, your baby is now strong enough to lift his legs in the air to look at them, and is likely to pop them into his mouth. He is also strong enough to reach out for toys and has got more accurate when reaching for and grabbing objects. This is aided by the fact that he has now developed depth perception, so he can see where things are in relation to one another. A baby at this age often loves to bounce. When you hold him upright he appears to bounce on your lap, as if he is trying to jump. This is a great way to let him strengthen his legs without having to hold his own body weight.

How to help

- Promote tummy time so that he can practise lifting his head and chest and putting his weight on his arms. Initially you can help by placing him on his front over a small bolster to allow him to feel the position.
- Get down on the floor with him and make it a game; encourage him to roll around with you, rewarding him with a kiss or a tickle.
- Move some toys and encourage him to roll towards them.
- Show him the world from a new perspective: sitting up! Make sure he can reach toys from a sitting position or read books to him.
- Allow time on his back in loose clothing to give him space to kick and strengthen his legs. He may love doing this when he has his nappy changed and is free from the sensation of wearing a nappy.
- Let him bounce when holding him upright to help strengthen his legs.

Handling skills

Your baby uses his hands and fingers like a rake to pull objects towards him. Once he is able to reach for objects himself, he will also start to play with them. He will hold objects in a 'palmar grasp' – the object is held in his palm with his fingers wrapped around it, holding it tightly. He is able to release objects when he wants to, although it may take some convincing to encourage him to do so!

As he becomes more curious your baby will handle toys to see what they do, shaking a rattle or banging a toy on the floor. He will put everything he can get hold of into his mouth. His lips and tongue are full of nerve endings, making them really sensitive, so that they can give your baby lots of information about the object; what it feels like, its texture, shape and of course its taste. At this age it is recommended that you start weaning (see page 30), and so some of the things he puts in his mouth will actually be food!

Your baby will not show 'handedness' as yet: you should not be able to see if he is right- or left-handed. If you do think that he favours one side, you should consult your doctor. Instead of favouring one side your baby is learning about both sides of his body; he will bang toys together, clap his hands together and transfer toys from one hand to the other.

How to help
- Use a wide variety of toys and shakers to allow him to experience different shapes and textures. These do not have to be expensive; a wooden spoon to bang on the floor or a saucepan is an old favourite!
- Encourage him to pass objects from one hand to the other.
- Play games where you hold a toy on one side and allow him to grab it, and then try from the other side.

Speech and language

By now your baby will be babbling away making repetitive cooing sounds such as 'aaaaa' and 'oooh'. He will look closely at your face when you are talking to him and may be able to respond to some facial expressions or tones of voice; for example, he may appear frightened or upset by loud voices or shouting. He can distinguish between a friendly voice and an angry one. You may be able to have your first conversations with your baby; you talk to him and he burbles or coos back. He will start to give long soliloquies and look at you expectantly for an answer when he has finished: these are the beginnings of conversation! He will start to use different sounds to show different emotions in order to communicate with you.

Your baby is often fascinated by the sounds he can make and shows real pleasure at being able to communicate and make noises that are not crying. You may find that he really enjoys squealing or shouting, and makes the noises over and over again. He will also start to make growling or clicking sounds, and start to blow bubbles or smack his lips together, all of which help to develop the muscles required for speech.

During the 6 to 9 month period, you may notice that the cooing sounds develop into more babbling sounds with a consonant and vowel used together, such as 'babababab' or 'dadadada'. He may say 'mama' or 'dada' but this is likely to be a sound that he can say and enjoys saying, rather than him using it to mean 'Mummy' or 'Daddy' – but do not worry, it will not be long until he can associate the meaning!

How to help
- Talk, read and sing to him!
- Let him look at your face when you speak so that he can see your mouth move and watch your facial expressions at the same time. Much of communication is non-verbal, so allowing him to watch your face will help him to learn the non-verbal cues.
- Play making funny faces, like big smiles, wide open mouth or pursed lips; you may find that he starts to copy you!
- Try having a conversation with him: ask a question and wait for a response. If you get a conversation, keep going! The conversation does not have to be in words; you can copy him by saying 'bababa' and then he may respond by saying the same.

Social and emotional development

Your baby has now begun to start to make sense of what he feels, so he learns to understand what it feels like to be hungry or full, or to have a wet nappy, and will use his developing communication skills to try to tell you how he feels. Of course this may be by crying, but you may be able to distinguish one kind of cry or call from another as he tries to tell you want he wants. He also has an idea that he wants things, such as a toy or a cuddle, and will be quite determined to get them.

For example, if he wants the green rattle rather than the blue rattle he will start to push away the blue rattle, or if he does pick it up he may drop the blue one until he gets the green. He learns this because you help him to understand his feelings and desires: when he is hungry you feed him, when he is wet you change him and when he needs comfort you cuddle and croon to him, so he begins to makes sense of how he is feeling.

When he wants to be lifted up, your baby will start to lift his arms up to you. He can also follow simple directions such as 'arms up' or 'clap hands'. He is learning his name, and will turn or respond to being called his name. This often starts with his responding to the sound of you calling any word in the tone in which you call his name (so you may find he turns to being called 'hairbrush', for example!); however, he will soon learn to turn only to the sound of his own name. He will start to look for a person familiar to him if you ask him, such as 'Where is Daddy?'.

At this age your baby tends to be extremely sociable and friendly, and happy to babble and play with others. He becomes aware of, and recognises, the most important people in his world, namely you, and will show that he recognises you by being happy to see you. As he realises how important you are, he can also begin to become more aware of strangers, and may be more anxious or less playful with strangers. (For further information on separation anxiety, see Chapter 4.) He will show you that he enjoys being played with or talked to by laughing and smiling and talking back, and you may find him practising these skills by making faces in a mirror or copying your facial expressions.

It is recommended that you start weaning at 6 months old, meaning that your baby starts to eat solid food. There are various methods to start weaning your baby. One method involves mashing or liquidising the food to a near-liquid consistency, and then slowly increasing the amount of texture. Another method is called 'baby-led weaning', whereby you give him whole foods, such as pieces of soft-boiled carrot or pieces of cheese, and he learns to chew and mash the food up himself in his mouth. Many parents use a combination of the two methods; for example, spoon feeding some baby rice or fruit puree, as well as giving your baby a piece of fruit or a soft-cooked vegetable to chew on himself.

Initially you will find that your baby may not appear to know what to do with a mouthful of food. He spits it straight out again, it gets smeared around his mouth, and it can feel like more is on his face, clothes and the floor than he actually swallows! This is because the action of sucking, be it on a nipple or a bottle, is actually quite different to the action required to pull food off a spoon, keep it inside his mouth, chew it if required and then transfer it to the back of his mouth for swallowing. As with everything, this takes practice and you will find that your baby does get more efficient at eating. He is used to the thin, watery texture of milk and it takes time to learn to adjust to thicker fluids, purees and foods with different textures and sensations in the mouth. Importantly, he is also learning that some things are food and that some things are not!

Your baby will start to use his developing handling skills to pick up or hold his water cup and to transfer food to his mouth using his hands or even a spoon (though the food may fall off it before it gets to his mouth!). You may also notice that he starts to hold the bottle himself at around 6 to 10 months old. At first, this is just a hand or two on the bottle to help you, but eventually he will be strong enough to hold the weight of it on his own. Even if he can hold the bottle himself, do not leave him alone to do so, or prop the bottle in his mouth, due to the risk of choking. Instead, use the time for cuddles!

How to help

- Cuddles, playing and talking! Games such as clapping or tickling, or copying funny faces such as sticking your tongue out.
- Talk to him. Ask him what he wants when he is crying and when you have found the answer, such as a dirty nappy, explain to him that he may have been crying because he felt uncomfortable in a wet or dirty nappy. This may help him to further understand his feelings.
- Be understanding that he may be anxious around less familiar people, even if this is a grandparent, and that he may need cuddles and reassurance.
- Play games such as 'Where Is?': first touch your nose and say 'Here is Mummy's nose, where is Mummy's nose?', then let him grab your nose, and then show him his nose on himself.

- Let him start to feed himself, with some finger foods when he is able and also by letting him hold the spoon, with and then without, your help. This encourages him to develop the coordination needed to pick up food and get it into his mouth. It is the first step towards him being able to feed himself.
- Start to use a cup for drinks of water at mealtimes so he can start to develop the skill of drinking from a cup as opposed to a nipple or bottle.
- Eat with him, show him how you eat and hold a spoon, even making exaggerated chewing faces can all help to show him how one eats!

Problem solving

At 6 to 9 months old, your baby will start to play with objects for longer periods of time, because he is able to concentrate for 2 to 3 minutes at a time. He will also begin to develop an idea of 'object permanence'; this is when he realises that even though he cannot see an object, it still exists. If you partially cover up a toy, he understands that the rest of that toy still exists and so he will try to uncover the toy or pull it out. As his understanding progresses, you can put two rattles or toys in front of your baby, and then make a show of removing one, putting it behind your baby's back. He will twist to try to see where you have put it, showing that he understands that the rattle still exists, even though he cannot see it.

This idea of object permanence leads your baby towards understanding that you, his parent, can disappear for a short period and come back again. However, he does not have an understanding of time and so may get distressed when you leave the room because he knows that you are important and he is not sure when, or if, you will come back again.

How to help

- Play dropping and picking-up games. You can drop or hide a toy and then make it reappear, much to his delight! Encourage him to drop the toy and then you can magically make it reappear simply by picking it up!
- Partially hide a toy, for example by putting a muslin or a piece of paper over a toy so he can still see some of it, and encourage him to uncover it – 'Ta dah!'.
- He will love to play Peek-a-boo. Not only does this have the frisson of the momentary fear of your disappearance followed very shortly by the joy of your reappearance, but it also helps your baby to understand that although you may go away, you always come back.

Should I worry? Is my child developing correctly?

See your doctor when your baby is 9 months old if:

- he cannot hold up his head
- he cannot sit up unaided
- he is very floppy or very stiff
- he does not seem to respond to you in any way (for example, no response to noises or smiles)
- he does not seem to recognise you or seem pleased to see you
- he does not reach for toys
- he does not turn towards sounds
- he does not look towards an object or a person at which you are pointing
- he does not make any sounds.

You should also see your doctor if your baby loses a skill which he previously had, for example he was making sounds or holding up his head, but then stops doing so.

4

9–12 months

Mobility

Here we go! You probably spent some of the last few months wondering when your baby will get moving and are now rushing around baby-proofing your house, as most babies tend to start crawling at this age. There are various different crawling techniques. A baby may start on his hands and knees, rocking himself back and forth to strengthen the muscles needed for crawling, and then one day will crawl in this position. Another baby will 'commando crawl': here he lies on his front and uses his arms to pull himself along the floor, just like a soldier pulls himself along through the undergrowth. Yet do not worry if your baby does not crawl. A baby might skip crawling altogether, going straight to standing, or he might roll over and over to get to where he is going. He may adopt the 'bottom shuffle': here he sits on his bottom and then scoots along the floor using one or both legs to propel himself along. The method by which your baby chooses to get around does not make a difference as long as he is showing signs of moving around in some manner. Whichever technique your baby chooses, he will develop confidence and speed. He may also attempt to crawl up the stairs, so keep an eye open and perhaps use a stair gate to prevent accidents.

Your baby will now be a confident sitter. He can sit unaided with a straight back, and may attempt to pull himself up to standing. By holding on to furniture or your hands, he may be able to stand. He may even be able to stand unsupported for a few seconds, before bumping back down onto the floor! When standing and holding on, he may attempt a few steps: this is known as 'cruising'. Your baby may have the balance and muscle control to attempt to pick something up from the floor, leaving him holding on with only one hand.

At around this age your baby will develop a new reflex, called the 'parachute' reflex. Here, if your baby is held in the upright position and then turned quickly to face the floor as if he is going to fall, he will put out his arms, as if to break the fall (see Figure 4). This reflex persists into adulthood.

Baby walkers were thought to be a toy that helped a baby to walk. However, many professionals now discourage their use because walkers can cause accidents and injuries. A baby walker allows

Figure 4

him extra height (to reach things that are potentially dangerous), and the wheels allow extra speed. Injuries can be caused by the walker tipping over with a baby inside. It may be that these walkers slow down walking development: a baby learns to walk after rolling, sitting and crawling, all of which build up the muscles required for walking. Baby walkers are best avoided: it is safer to let him play on the floor.

How to help

- Make moving fun! He will love to crawl to Mummy, with a big cuddle or a tickle as a reward.
- Move toys just slightly out of his reach so that he has to move to get them, but avoid letting him get too frustrated and cross if he cannot reach. (Have a go – but give the toy back if he cannot manage it!)
- Hold his hands when he is standing to encourage him to take a few steps – but do not worry if he does not want to move.

Handling skills

From around 4 months old, your baby has grasped objects with the whole fist, known as the 'palmar grasp'. Towards the end of the first year he will develop a 'pincer grasp' whereby he can use his thumb and first finger to pick up small objects. At 1 year old you may notice that he starts to use one hand more than the other but you cannot truly tell if he is going to be right- or left-handed for another year or so. He will be able to pick up objects of different sizes by now, dropping them when he wants to, transferring them between his hands and banging them together. At this age he will also learn to clap his hands. As he develops more control over his fingers, he will learn to point and use that skill to show you what he wants. By about 1 year old your baby will be able to hold a crayon, often in the palmar grasp, and if you show him how, he may be able to apply enough pressure to do a scribble on some paper.

How to help

- Give him different objects to feel and explore. For example, small plastic storage containers filled with different objects such as dried pasta; or a plastic spoon; or small blocks that can be moved into different-sized containers.
- Show him how to move small objects from one container into another, or how to fill up a container and then tip everything out again.
- Let him use objects of different sizes so that he can practise both his palmar grasp and pincer grasp. Mealtimes can be a great opportunity: for dessert, give him some apple slices and raisins; he may pick up the apple using his whole fist but may have a go at picking up the raisins using a pincer motion.
- Introduce sensory sessions. For example, fill different containers with various objects to touch and feel, such as rice, material, wool and beans, or items from the garden such as leaves, twigs or pine cones. He will love to feel the different textures.
- Encourage water play. Even a simple jug or two in the bath can instigate sensory play and develop motor skills in the handling of, and pouring with, jugs.

Speech and language

It is towards the end of the first year that your baby will start to show that he understands you and will start to communicate with you, using mainly non-verbal communication, such as gestures and facial expressions, rather than words. He knows that words have meaning and will look at the right picture or object when you name it. He understands simple requests such as 'come to Mummy' or 'pick up teddy', and he uses gestures or signs, for example waving bye-bye, nodding and shaking his head, and pointing to objects that he wants. He may even be able to respond to a question such as 'Where is your head?' by pointing at it. Although he may understand 'no' he may choose to ignore you, especially if he hears the word 'no' repeatedly. Try using 'no' only when he is doing something which is potentially dangerous and in other situations use different language (for example, if he is getting mucky and you don't want him to, don't say 'no, don't do that', rather try 'please stop putting mud on your hair'), or distract him with a new activity. He also understands the tone of your voice, so speaking in a low tone or crossly, or in a higher, excited voice, will give him clues as to what you mean.

His verbal speech is also changing, with the earlier babbling sounds becoming sounds that are more speech-like in their tone, such as his voice going up if he is excited. He may say a stream of sounds that copy the rhythm of language: you say a sentence and he may copy by babbling, but with the same rhythm and intonation of what you originally said. The babble of 'mamamama' and 'dadadada' now changes to 'mama' and 'dada', which begin to be used to mean 'Mummy' and 'Daddy'. Mums should not be upset if 'dada' comes first: it is simply easier to say! Some meaningful noises may start to appear, such as 'ooh' for something exciting or 'uh-oh' for something going wrong, and he may have a particular noise for something such as a favourite toy. Your baby will try to copy words you say such as 'hello', which often becomes 'e-oh'. He may also attempt a sibling's name.

How to help

- Help him to make the connection between words and meaning by naming things as you give them to him, or pointing to objects in pictures and naming them.
- Read simple books to him, pointing to the pictures and talking about what you can see. Do not just read the words in the book, but make it more of a fluid conversation.
- Talk to him and with him all the time. Sing nursery rhymes and give a running commentary on what you are doing. Ask him questions such as 'Would you like to wear the red top or the green one?' or 'Would you like peas or corn for lunch?', and show him both choices. At some point he will answer: even if he only points, he is still developing language skills as he is communicating with you.
- Help him to understand simple instructions by using gestures. For example, if you want him to 'Bring your bowl', point to the bowl at the same time as speaking. Keep the instructions very simple with only one action at a time; for example, 'Bring your bowl' instead of 'Bring your bowl and put it on the table'.

Social and emotional development

Although your baby has been very sociable, you may notice that as he gets older, he becomes shy and displays nervous and clingy behaviour towards parents and carers when meeting strangers or in new surroundings. Your baby may have separation anxiety and may cry when you leave a room. This is because he now understands who you are and that you are important to him but has no concept of time and does not know if or when you will come back again. He may also show that something scares him (for example, having his hair washed) and may cling to you or cry in these situations.

By using his developing language skills, your baby can communicate with you, and you may have learnt what certain sounds or gestures signify. He initiates play by fetching a toy, or he may get a book that he wishes you to read. He can now play simple games such as Peek-a-boo: the momentary anxiety that you have gone mixes with the thrill of your coming back! Your baby now has control of his hands, so will play clapping games such as Pat-a-cake and can wave bye-bye. Music is a favourite activity: your baby will often clap, bounce or bop along when music is on. You may also find that he helps you when you are getting him dressed by holding out an arm or a leg.

At mealtimes, your baby will begin to feed himself finger foods, but be prepared for lots of mess as he enjoys himself. By 9 months old, he can get the food from his hand into his mouth with ease (in fact, more easily than by using cutlery), but by the time he is 1 year old, he may be able to start using a spoon. When your baby starts to use a spoon he can take, for example, some yoghurt onto the spoon but he turns it over before it gets to his mouth, generally dropping most of it onto the table, and he then puts the upside-down spoon into his mouth. With a bit of practice, his spoon-handling skills improve and he can transfer the spoon the correct way up into his mouth. At this age, your baby will enjoy eating foods with a wide variety of textures, whether or not he has many teeth. You should try to introduce lots of different flavours and textures into his food and see what he likes and dislikes. He can curve his lips around the rim of a cup to drink, and he can also hold the cup, though he will need help as a cup of liquid is heavy. He may even be able to drink through a straw. Mealtimes are a great opportunity for communicating with your baby and noticing that he is also communicating with you: he may reach for or point to food when he is hungry, get excited when he sees food and show that he is full by pushing the food away or shaking his head.

At this age, your baby does not have any concept of safety and may appear fearless about things that could be dangerous, such as stairs or plug sockets. Although he knows what you mean when you say 'no', he does not understand why he should obey, or even that he should follow your instructions at all. He is not being defiant; he is simply trying to understand and explore the world around him. You will have to repeat the same instructions many times because he will not necessarily remember tomorrow that you told him not to play with the plug socket 20 times today. You will need to set your boundaries and stick to them. By you being consistent, your baby begins to learn what is expected of him and which behaviours are not acceptable.

Despite some separation anxiety, your baby will be contented and happy at this age: indeed, he may have a great sense of humour. He will smile at you when you enter the room, and he loves to play interactive games and laugh with you. Your baby thinks that you can be hilariously funny and will giggle if you pull funny faces, play Peek-a-boo or tickle him.

Attachment to a particular toy, blanket or rag is very common. This 'comfort blanket' (which may not be a blanket!) is called a 'transitional object' and is used for comfort at a time when your baby is learning to become independent. The object is generally chosen at around 6 months to 1 year old, but once it is chosen he is likely to remain attached to it for a period of years. It may be used to help him to get to sleep, and to comfort him when he is upset. The object is often soft, fluffy or smooth and it gives comfort because it is familiar and feels safe; it smells like home or his bed. Your baby may carry the object around with him and may like to stroke it over and over, rub it over his face, or suck on it. Having a comfort blanket is not a sign of an emotional problem; it is a common part of development which can help to comfort your baby or to settle him as part of his bedtime routine.

How to help

- Offer comfort if he is showing fear and anxiety, even if you know that there is nothing to be afraid of. Try modelling, where you show him that you are not afraid: for example, of having water poured on you.
- Introduce a consistent goodbye routine. If he has separation anxiety, a certain quick song or phrase followed by a kiss and cuddle may help. Do not make the goodbye last too long and do not go back to him if you hear him crying (which may confuse him because he thinks crying will bring you back for more cuddles).
- Rest assured that a few minutes or even seconds after you have gone, he will be fine. He will soon learn that although it feels like you have disappeared, you will always come back! There are many parents who leave a crying baby and stand outside the nursery door (often crying themselves), only to hear him settle down after a few minutes.
- Help him to be independent by letting him explore another room in your home on his own for a few minutes (as long as it is safe).
- Set consistent rules and boundaries – and keep repeating yourself.
- Buy another identical comfort object to the one he has chosen. Having two relieves the pressure if one goes missing briefly and allows for washing them. However, your child is canny and will soon learn the difference between the well-loved (and therefore careworn and with a familiar scent) and the brand new object. To avoid this it is worth swapping them over very regularly!
- Play simple games such as Peek-a-boo or role-playing games such as tea parties (making tea for each other and for teddies). Sing to him and listen to music together, dancing and enjoying the rhythms. Also sing nursery rhymes with actions, such as 'This little piggy' or 'Round and round the garden'. This helps with both his social development and his language skills.
- Encourage him with the dressing process by asking for help by saying, for example, 'Please can you give Mummy your arm?'. This can be a game, and once he knows where his limbs are, you can try joking: say 'Here is your leg' when holding his arm, and then laugh and say 'It's not your leg, silly Mummy'.

- Give him finger foods at mealtimes to help improve his hand to mouth coordination and handling skills. Let him get messy: lay a mat down underneath his high chair, and buy a pelican bib (a bib with a scoop at the bottom to catch all the dropped pieces of food) and lots of baby wipes. Also let him try to use a spoon. You can take it in turns with the 'one spoon from me and one spoon from you' routine to ensure that at least some food makes it into his mouth.

Problem solving

As your baby becomes more mobile, his world enlarges, giving him so much more to explore. Everything and anything is interesting and will be picked up and examined. He will still use his mouth to feel things, but will also use his hands and even try other methods of assessment. For example, he may bang things together, try to shake them, lick them, taste them, throw them, push them and knock them over. He enjoys activities such as putting things into containers and taking them out again. He will give you a toy as well as taking a toy from you, though he does not yet understand sharing.

By now your baby has an understanding of 'object permanence', which means that he understands that things exist even though he cannot see them. This leads to a game which he loves but you may find extremely frustrating! For example, when your baby is sitting in his high chair, he throws an object such as his spoon onto the floor. You pick it up and give it back and straight away he throws it back down again, and the pattern is repeated ... over and over and over. He is delighted each time you return the spoon, and if you do not give it back, he shows you that he knows it is still there by leaning over the side of his high chair looking for it, or making a noise calling you to bring it back. This is called 'casting' and means that he will start to look for a hidden object and may even look for something where he knows he has hidden it (but he will not understand where it has gone if you move it when he is not looking).

Towards the end of the first year your baby has enough understanding of the world to be able to know what particular objects are for and to use them correctly. So he will attempt to brush his hair with a hairbrush, and his teeth with a toothbrush. He will find it hilarious if you use something out of context, such as pretending to brush his teeth with a hairbrush.

How to help

- Let him explore! Make sure your home is safe and baby-proof and then let him loose. He may open cupboards, so you could leave a cupboard full of things for him to explore such as a light saucepan, plastic boxes, a wooden spoon and a shaker. He can then work out what he can do with them. To an 11-month-old baby everything is exciting; everything is a potential toy and needs thorough investigation.
- Encourage him to enjoy taking toys or objects out of a container, proving that he knows that something is in there!
- Join in with his casting games. Every time you pick up the toy, you are showing him that it still exists even though he dropped it!

Should I worry? Is my child developing correctly?

See your doctor when your baby is 1 year old if:

- he is not sitting unaided
- he is not crawling or moving around at all
- he does not make any babbling noises
- he does not turn towards sounds
- he does not make any eye contact
- he does not seem to recognise you or show pleasure at seeing familiar people
- he appears to be right- or left-handed, or seems to list to one side, or drags one side when crawling
- he does not use gestures, such as pointing or shaking his head.

You should also see your doctor if your baby loses a skill which he previously had; for example he was pointing or saying a word, but then stops doing so.

5

12–18 months

Mobility

By now your baby is moving around in some manner, be it 'commando crawling', crawling on his hands and knees, rolling or bottom shuffling. He is able to transfer himself from a sitting to a crawling position and is able to crawl up the stairs. At first, climbing up is easier than climbing back down again, but in time you can show him how to turn around and crawl down the stairs backwards on his tummy, or bump down on his bottom.

At around 1 year old, your baby will begin to pull himself up to a standing position by holding on to the furniture or your hands and pulling himself upright. He will then begin to 'cruise' round the furniture, holding on to support and balance himself. Next, he can take a few steps holding on to your hands or fingers. Once he is practised at standing by holding on, he will begin to stand for a few seconds unsupported, before falling down on his bottom. Before you know it he will start walking alone! When your toddler first starts to toddle, you will notice that he places his feet very wide apart and has his hands up for balance. As he further develops the skill of walking he will gradually bring his feet closer together. If your baby is not walking by the time he is 18 months old, you should see your doctor. However, this does not necessarily mean that something is wrong; for example, it is known that a baby who is a bottom shuffler (who moves around sitting up by shuffling forwards on his bottom) often walks at a later age.

As time progresses, your baby will be able to stand up without holding on to anything, and will then be strong enough to squat and play with toys from a squatting position. He will then start to walk up the stairs holding your hand, initially putting both feet on each step (so if he steps up onto the first step with his right foot, he will then bring up his left foot onto the same step, and not onto the step above, before moving up to the next step in the same manner). As he becomes stronger and more adventurous, you will notice that your baby begins to scramble up onto the sofa or a chair. Once he is confident with walking he will be able to kick a ball, not by standing on one leg and kicking it, but by walking into it and then following after it again, although he begins to understand the concept of running after a ball and then making the ball move further away.

While your baby is still finding his feet it is best to leave him without shoes, although you can use socks to keep his feet warm. This is because he needs to be able to feel the floor through his feet and use this feedback to help him to balance and then to walk. Try to avoid getting heavily soled shoes until he is a confident walker, and even then he may prefer to be barefoot when indoors. The bones in your toddler's feet are still very soft and malleable; going barefoot (or in socks) will allow his feet to develop without being restricted. Getting your toddler's first pair of shoes is a milestone in his life, but do not be surprised if he is unhappy or upset about wearing them. It is a big change to suddenly have relatively heavy objects strapped onto your feet, and your toddler may well express his dislike of shoes to you! Once he is ready for shoes, be sure to have his feet measured and his shoes fitted by a professional to ensure a good fit. First shoes should be supportive, with straps or fastenings to hold them securely in place, and with a flexible sole. Ideally his shoes will be made of a breathable material such as leather or canvas because plastic shoes can make his feet sweat, which may make the shoes feel slippery and may increase the chances of athlete's foot developing (which is a fungal infection of the skin of the feet). After the excitement of the first shoe fitting it is recommended that you take your toddler to have his feet checked approximately every 8 weeks, as his feet will grow quickly and he may have grown out of his first shoes before you know it!

How to help
- Give him plenty of freedom to crawl around and pull himself up using the furniture. Do not force him to walk until he is ready.
- Baby-proof your house before he gets into everything! You may wish to consider stair gates or plug-socket covers. However, no matter how well baby-proofed your house may be, he will be extremely ingenious at getting things which interest him, so be sure to keep an eye on him!
- Let him go barefoot and experience different textures through his feet: soft, warm carpet, cool lino or tiles and the earth or mud between his toes.
- Make moving a game. Once he is walking, you can play games such as placing two containers a short distance apart, and then asking him to take the toys out of one container and to walk to the other container to put the toy there. Reward any achievement with smiles and cheers – it may only be a few steps but to him this is a big deal!

Handling skills

Your toddler's pincer grip will be developing so that he is able to pick up objects with increasing dexterity. He may be able to help you turn the pages of a book; board books are good for this as the pages are made of thick cardboard, making them easier to get hold of than books made of paper. He will enjoy lifting flaps in books: not only is this great fun, but it also practises the pincer grip, and helps him to develop the idea of object permanence (that something which is hidden still exists).

The development of his handling skills means that your toddler is starting to place shapes in the relevant shaped hole in a shape-sorter toy. Initially, you may need to show him which shape fits in which hole, but with time he will start to try all the holes for himself. He understands that the shapes go into the holes and will try to turn the shapes around to fit them in the slot. Give him encouragement, with lots of cheers and smiles when he pops the correct shape in the hole! You can also talk around games such as these: talk about the colours, the shapes and how they may feel. With time, he can play with these toys with minimal help, just as you improve at any task with practice. He will also start to be able to stack blocks and by 18 months old he is able to make a tower of three bricks.

Your toddler is able to start making marks on paper: he may enjoy finger painting or scribbling with crayons. Loving bright colours, he may prefer to use large round-tipped felt pens or crayons rather than pencils because they do not require as much pressure to make a bright scribble on the page. You should encourage his mark making: it is the beginnings of writing!

How to help
- Give him time to practise his pincer grip. For example, lifting flaps in books, turning book pages and picking up small objects such as Cheerios™ cereal (even though it may take him a long time to eat his snack in this manner!).
- Encourage mark making in various ways, from finger painting to scribbling with crayons. Do not worry about what it is he produces; it is the act itself which is important. Ask him about what he has drawn: he may well tell you!
- Offer him toys and objects with different textures so that he can explore the sense of touch.

Speech and language

At about 1 year old your toddler is likely to be able to say a few words. He now uses 'mama' and/or 'dada' with real meaning because he understands that words have meaning and are not simply sounds. However, non-verbal communication is also used: he will make noises such as 'yay' or 'uh-oh' and will use gestures such as waving bye-bye or nodding/shaking his head. Instead of crying, your toddler will make noises to grab your attention, and he can show you what he wants; for example, picking up a book when he wants a story. His facial expression will also tell you lots about what he is feeling.

You may find that the babbling sounds your toddler makes begin to sound more like speech because they copy the cadence and rhythm of speech. He tries to say words, and by 18 months old he can say some words, but it is his understanding that has developed significantly. He can now understand questions and can answer them, perhaps not by using words, but in his actions. For example, he will understand and follow an instruction if you ask him to get his teddy from the kitchen, or ask him to give you his beaker. He may be able to identify a body part, and will show you by pointing to the relevant part when you ask him 'Where is your head?'.

How to help

- As always, keep talking! It does not matter if he does not understand every word that you say; just keep talking and he will soon pick it up. When you are playing, talk to him about it; when you are talking to a friend, include him in the conversation as he will be listening; and when you are listening to some music, sing along.
- Show that you consider his speech important. Get down to his height to talk to him, which helps you to pick up the non-verbal cues in his facial expression so that you can work out what it is he is saying.
- Sing songs with pointing actions, such as 'Heads, shoulders, knees and toes'.
- Read books, point to the pictures and talk around the subject of the book as well as reading the story itself. For example, if you are reading a farm book, when you see a picture of a duck, stop and tell him it is a duck and ask him what the duck says; initially, you will have to tell him that the duck says 'quack', but soon he will tell you.

Social and emotional development

Although you are still dressing and undressing him, your toddler is now able to partake in the process. He starts by being able to pull off his shoes and socks (previously, your toddler may have pulled off his socks just because he could, for fun, but now he does it when you ask him to). He now not only holds out a limb to help with dressing, but understands to push his arms and legs through the relevant holes in his clothing.

Your toddler is likely to show separation anxiety. This is when he becomes upset and cries when you, as his parent, leave him. This may happen when you leave to go to work, or even if you just leave to go to another room or leave his bedroom at night. You may notice that he follows you everywhere, even to the toilet! This is because he realises how important you are in his world but does not yet understand that you will come back again. Even when he does begin to understand that you will return, he still does not know when that will be and he does not yet have a concept of time, so he does not grasp if you will be gone for minutes or hours, or even how long a minute or an hour is!

You may find that your toddler cries every morning when you leave for work but that when you come home his carer tells you that the tears dried up within a few minutes. Therefore it may be best not to prolong your goodbyes when you are leaving, or to keep coming back when he cries because this will make it harder for him to understand what is happening. Yet you should not avoid the goodbye altogether because your toddler will eventually realise that you have gone and may become distressed at that point. Instead, explain to him what is happening, that you are leaving to go to work, that X is looking after him, and that Mummy will be back later – and do not forget your kiss or cuddle! Of course it is hard to see your toddler upset and it is common to feel sad or guilty. The tearful goodbye can have tears from both parent and toddler, but you should try not to show your upset in front of your toddler as this may distress him further.

Another example of your toddler's understanding of your importance in his life is that he becomes nervous or shy around strangers and anxious in new situations and environments. This may manifest itself as 'clingy' behaviour. Just as he has favourite people, he may also have favourite toys and may become very attached to a particular object, toy or stuffed animal, dragging it around with him and sleeping with it. He may show obvious affection towards his toys, hugging them, or if he is eating he may try to feed them. This is the beginning of role play, often initially copying what he has seen you do with him.

Your toddler can play simple games with you, still enjoying Peek-a-boo, clapping games such as Pat-a-cake, and giving a 'high-five'. However, he will not yet be able to play with other children: he may play next to them, or he may ignore them and get on with what he wants to do. He is not yet able to share and does not understand about taking turns with a toy: why should he give up something which he is enjoying to let someone else have a turn? As such, if another toddler is playing with something he wants he may go over to try to take it away. You will find that you will explain about sharing over and over again. Even many adults are not good at sharing, but your toddler at this age may become very cross or upset about having to share. Although he is not yet able to understand the concept of sharing, and that he should not snatch, you will show him (over and over) with your tone of voice and your words what is acceptable behaviour, and what is unacceptable.

You may notice that your toddler is easily frustrated: he knows what he wants but cannot always express himself to get his needs met. This means that he may start to have tantrums, but as his language skills develop, these will (hopefully!) decrease. You may feel frustrated with him when he is having a tantrum that is difficult to stop; perhaps this is a reflection of his frustration. When he is having a tantrum, it may help to empathise with your toddler, 'I can see that you're frustrated that Mummy doesn't know what you want'. Offer lots of cuddles but remain firm about inappropriate behaviour such as biting or hitting. It is understandably exasperating for you when your toddler has a meltdown, lying on the floor in the middle of a playgroup, but just understanding the cause (for example, he is frustrated at being asked to share when he cannot comprehend why) may help you respond to the situation in a calm manner. Admittedly this can sometimes be difficult!

When eating, your toddler is becoming increasingly independent: he can feed himself with a spoon without turning it over before it gets to his mouth! He is able to drink from a cup and through a straw. When you are out and about he may use a cup with a lid for ease, but at home he is starting to use an ordinary cup. Eating is a social skill and he will enjoy eating with you and all the interaction that it involves. He also loves to experience new and different smells, flavours and textures in his food.

How to help

- Attend playgroups. It may seem easier to avoid playgroups if he finds it difficult to share, but attending playgroups and mixing with other children is the first step towards socialising and it can be helpful for you to meet other parents. Your local library or Sure Start centre may have some free or inexpensive playgroups and are good places to interact with other children and parents.
- Encourage him to be more independent, even if it means that everyday activities take longer or become more messy. For example, ask him to put his arms up to put on his top, and let him feed himself even if some goes on the floor or he tips over his drink. These skills take practice!
- Introduce him to new situations while keeping the familiarity of the old. For instance, if you take him to a new playgroup allow him to stay close to you until he finds his confidence.

Problem solving

There are many signs that your toddler's problem-solving skills are developing. As you read a book together, he looks at an object if you point to it, or if you talk about it. He knows the use of an object, such as a toothbrush, and may start to role play, brushing teddy's teeth. He starts to copy you and your actions, so if he sees you brushing your hair, he will try to do the same.

Your toddler learns to point. He can point to a body part on your request and point to something he wants (called the 'protoimperative point' – for example, if he wants a drink he will point to his cup). This develops into his pointing at something to show it to you (called the 'protodeclarative point'). He may pull at your clothing or make a noise to get your attention before pointing at an object. This shows that he understands that he can point not only to get something, but also to show you something that interests him, which is part of your two-way relationship (he finds something interesting and so wants to show you).

Your toddler continues to explore and learn about the world, mostly via his senses. Everything is fascinating, from a crumb on the floor to the patterns made by the leaves on a tree fluttering in the wind. Letting him explore his environment encourages him to learn: for example, a round object such as a ball will roll across the floor and a cube-shaped block will not; some objects bounce and others will not; and touching a particular toy makes it produce a noise or a light. Your toddler will love tactile sensory stimulation; the feel of playing with objects with different textures such as water or sand. You will notice that he may be fascinated by things that may not seem interesting to you, such as an ant meandering across the pavement, but allowing your toddler the time to watch, touch and feel helps him to absorb information about the world.

How to help

- Promote sensory play. He will enjoy playing with things he can feel, like water, sand, earth, rice, flour or shaving foam. Practise pouring with jugs, or transferring sand or rice with a spoon into a container and pouring it out again.
- Sing pointing songs. For example, pointing at me and you, or body parts or parts of the room.
- Help him with pointing by giving him choices. For example, lay out two pairs of socks – 'Do you want the green pair or the blue pair?', pointing to each in turn as you say the colour, and then ask him to point to the pair he wants.
- Encourage role play, mimicking the everyday activities that you do, such as brushing a doll's hair, making a play cup of tea or imaginary cooking.

Should I worry? Is my child developing correctly?

See your doctor when your toddler is 18 months old if:

- he is not standing
- he is not walking
- he does not make noises or use a couple of words
- he does not appear to understand what you are saying
- he does not copy you, or know the use of familiar objects
- he does not seem to be aware of, or mind, your absence.

You should also see your doctor if he loses a skill that he has previously mastered.

18–24 months

Mobility

When your toddler first starts to toddle, he will have a very wide gait. By placing his feet far apart with each step, he creates a triangle shape with his legs which has a wide base for balance. He will also hold up his arms for balance. Your toddler waddles, taking short quick steps: but over time he will gradually bring his legs together, and so he waddles slightly less!

Do not worry if your toddler appears to be bow-legged as he walks: this is normal and his legs will straighten as he gets older (although he may become knock-kneed for a period of time, generally around 3 years old: see Chapter 9). He may also have an in-toeing gait, where his feet turn inwards as he walks. He is likely to grow out of this as he gets older. Your toddler may start walking on tip-toes, but this also tends to disappear with age. Flat feet are also common and not a worry: your toddler's joints are very flexible and so the arches flatten when he stands up. There are also fatty pads in his feet which may be hiding his arches; get him to stand on tip-toe and you may be better able to see the arches in his feet.

With regards to gait, see your doctor if:

- you notice that he is bow-legged or knock-kneed on one side only
- he is still in-toeing at 2 years old
- he is still walking on tip-toes at 2 years old
- the in-toeing is so severe that he is tripping over his own feet

- he complains of pain in one leg
- he has a limp.

As your toddler improves and practises his walking skills, he may start to run at about his second birthday (though for some toddlers it will be much later). Running involves having both feet off the ground at the same time, as opposed to walking, when one foot is on the floor at all times.

Other mobility skills your toddler has mastered include: being able to walk while carrying a toy or other object; kicking a ball (though this is still achieved by running into it rather than actively kicking it); and picking up a ball and throwing it (though without real accuracy!). He can walk up and down stairs holding on to your hand, and by 2 years old he will be able to climb up the stairs holding on to the banister. Your toddler is still climbing the stairs one at a time, bringing both feet up onto the same step before attempting the next step, and climbing up is easier than climbing down (when he needs to crawl backwards or shuffle down on his bottom). Your toddler will also be able to sit on a four-wheeled ride-on toy and 'drive' by pushing with his feet. By 2 years old he can sit on a sturdy tricycle and attempt to push the pedals – he may be strong enough to power it for himself and ride around.

> ## How to help
> - Practise, practise, practise! Help him up and down the stairs, a few steps at a time, holding your hand and then the banister.
> - Encourage walking. He is likely to enjoy 'push-and-pull' toys, such as pushing a toy lawnmower or a toy mop, or pulling a toy wheeled animal on a string.
> - Play with balls. Sit on the floor with your legs open wide in front of you and practise rolling the ball to and from each other. Progress to standing up and throwing the ball back and forth, or kicking the ball.

Handling skills

In the second year of life you may notice that your toddler develops 'handedness'; you may be able to see if your child is becoming right- or left-handed. Do not worry if you cannot tell – it may not be obvious for a few years yet. Your toddler's handling skills continue to improve: he will be able to turn, twist and push knobs, so may be very interested in knobs which he should not touch, such as those on the oven! You may also notice that he begins to put things in his mouth less often as he uses his hands, eyes and/or ears to explore objects.

You may notice that as he continues to scribble on paper with crayons, towards your toddler's second birthday these scribbles may change from being very linear to becoming more circular in nature. His brick-building skills will improve and by the time he is 2 years old your toddler can build a tower of six blocks. He will also be able to play games that involve taking pegs or other objects out of a bag and putting them into another container, or games involving putting hoops on pegs.

How to help

- Complete simple wooden puzzles. These often come with small peg handles which will develop his pincer grip as well as helping with problem solving (working out which piece goes into which hole).
- Play building games with blocks, or stacking toys, or connecting blocks such as Duplo™.
- Encourage mark making with finger paints or chubby crayons.

Speech and language

At around this age your toddler will hit the 'vocabulary explosion' when he starts learning new words extremely rapidly. He still will not have enough words to describe everything he wants, so he may generalise (for example, any fruit may be 'apple', or any animal may be 'cat'), but this is a great opportunity to expand his vocabulary by correcting him (telling him that this particular animal is a cow, for example). Your toddler may be learning eight to ten new words per day. As he learns new words, he may mispronounce them (for example, 'nana' for 'banana'). You do not need to tell him that he is wrong; simply repeat with the correct pronunciation, 'You would like a banana?'. Do not worry if he stammers at this age, especially if he is excited, because he is just trying to get his words out faster than he can actually say them. By 2 years old, you will understand about half of what he says (or less for other people who see him less frequently).

At about 18 months old your toddler will start to refer to himself by his own name, and a few months later he will start to use 'me' or 'I'. He is likely to be confused between 'me', 'I' and 'you'. This is understandable because you call him 'you' all the time, as in 'Do *you* want a drink?', so it seems reasonable that he will use 'you' in this context; 'pick *you* up' to mean 'pick *me* up'. This difference will take time and practice to perfect!

Approaching his second birthday, your toddler is likely to have more words than you can remember to count (approximately 100 words). He will begin to join up words in two- or three-word sentences such as 'want drink'. His language becomes more precise as he links words together, progressing from pointing at the drink, to saying 'drink', then 'want drink', to 'me want drink', etc. As his expressive language (meaning the words which he says) improves, so does his receptive language (meaning his understanding). So he can now follow more complex instructions that involve remembering two things, such as 'Go into the kitchen and get your cup'.

How to help

- Sing songs. He loves music: listening, dancing and singing. He may not get all the words correct when he joins in with your singing, but he can gabble along with the correct intonation and rhythm.
- Use nursery rhymes. If you stop and leave the last word of a line out, he may fill in the gaps. For example, 'Incy Wincy spider climbed up the water . . .'; pause and he may say 'spout', or more likely 'pout'!
- Keep talking. Repeat the words he says with the correct pronunciation and expand his sentences. For example, if he says 'milk', or 'want milk', you reply with 'Would you like some milk?'. Not only does this help him to learn whole sentences, but it also reinforces the idea that he is communicating with you; he asked you for something and you understood.
- Read books. He will like rhyming books as he enjoys the cadence and rhythms of the words as much as the meaning. He also likes to read the same books over and over!

Social and emotional development

Your toddler will continue to help you with dressing and undressing, by pushing his limbs into his clothes, but as yet he is unlikely to be able to take off his trousers. He may have a good enough pincer grip to be able to use a zip (if you start it for him) and may enjoy zipping and unzipping his clothes.

As your toddler's handling skills improve, so do his abilities with cutlery. By 2 years old he is likely to be able to drink confidently from a cup and will be getting less messy with a fork and spoon. Although some food may still be dropped on the floor or in his lap, he will be getting less around his mouth and more actually in it! He may begin to become fussy with regards to his food, but try to keep his diet varied and interesting, perhaps by allowing him to dip food instead of using a fork for a change, for example dipping vegetables into hummus.

With familiar people, your toddler is very affectionate. He will show you that he is excited and happy to see you, but he may be clingy or anxious when introduced to new people. He is likely to still have separation anxiety (becoming anxious when you leave him because he has no understanding of when you will come back).

Your toddler is beginning to show some empathy, so he may get upset or concerned if he sees you or any siblings crying and may even join in. He also knows to look for your reaction, such as encouragement or warning, before trying something new. He is experiencing new feelings: pride ('*my* toy' or '*my* Mummy'), guilt (looking at you after he has done something he knows he should not, perhaps with embarrassment), fear, shame, sadness and excitement (which can be hugely tense); but he does not always have the words to express these emotions. His feelings can be overwhelming and can trigger tantrums or tears. If he is having a tantrum, encourage him to use his words and try to express how he is feeling: 'I can see that you're upset/frustrated – can you use your words to tell me what is wrong/what you would like/how I can help?'. If he cannot answer then you can still help him to identify his emotions by saying you can see he is upset, and a simple cuddle may help.

Frustration can sometimes happen because your toddler wants to do something that you do not want him to, or is not safe. For example, if he wants to put a toy in a plug socket, then you need to tell him that you can see he is upset with you because you do not want him to do it, and you are sorry that he is upset, but it is not safe. At this age, your toddler can often be distracted out of a tantrum, with an exciting song or game. Even though he is beginning to exert his wants over yours to become more independent, at this age your toddler is very eager to please and will love to help out by following simple instructions, such as to bring you an object.

As he begins to have an understanding of possessions, your toddler uses words to tell you that a toy is 'mine' (though he may get confused between the words 'mine' and 'yours'). Sharing is still difficult for your toddler: you may find that he hits or bites if another child takes his toy and he is frustrated. It is important to be firm and tell him that this behaviour is not acceptable, that 'we do not bite'. He will continue to play next to children, as opposed to playing with them cooperatively, but he may begin to involve other children in his play, kicking a ball or chasing after them.

At this age, your toddler is starting to become more confident to play alone for short periods of time. In fact, as his independence grows, you may notice that he is becoming more single minded and strong willed. He may not listen to you when he is concentrating on doing something else. This is not defiance: he is simply exploring, interested in something else and exerting his independence. You may notice that he gets frustrated and may even have a tantrum when you ask him to stop what he is doing. To avoid this, give him some warning: but he may not understand 'five more minutes', so try 'Once you finish that puzzle, it's time to go'.

Often a favourite word for your toddler is 'no'. You can try to foster his independence by allowing him to make little choices. For example, if he does not want to put socks on and you feel he should, give him a choice of the red or blue socks, holding up each pair, instead of overruling him entirely. Note that it can help him to narrow his choices down as he may find it too overwhelming to pick from ten pairs of socks. If he continues to say 'no', then be firm; 'You have to wear socks but you can choose the blue or the red'. This method helps him to feel independent and yet you have still achieved the goal of him wearing socks. It may also be worth giving in to some small battles, so that he sometimes feels in control and develops an idea of his own self-worth – that his opinion is worth listening to.

How to help

- Encourage him to feed himself and use mealtimes as an opportunity to talk, helping him to engage in the social side of mealtimes.
- Let him socialise at a playgroup, library or with your friends. He may play next to other children, rather than with them, and he may struggle with sharing and turn taking, but exposure to other children and the expectations of social behaviour will help to teach him how to respond to, and interact with, other children.
- Allow him to make choices, such as which toy to play with or which plate to put his food on.

Problem solving

Your toddler's understanding of the world continues to develop and his language matures to show you how much he understands. He knows many body parts and can point to them when you ask, even if he cannot say the word himself. He may begin to be able to sort objects by colour or shape, although he may not know all the words: initially, he will learn only a few bright colours or simple shapes – do not expect him to understand the difference between a hexagon and an octagon! He will also be able to point to simple things in a book, such as an animal.

Using all his senses, your toddler continues to learn about the world by exploring, and also by copying you. Your toddler loves role play and will spend hours making you cups of tea, or pretending to feed a stuffed toy. This helps him to process the actions that he sees you doing on a daily basis and also gives him the opportunity to play a different role; for example, you may see your toddler wagging his finger at his teddy to tell him off!

You may notice that your toddler begins to show fear at this age: commonly of water, loud noises and other people. For example, he may become very distressed when it is time to wash his hair. He may not like the feeling of water on his head or over his face and he now has enough memory and understanding to know what is going to happen when you reach for the shampoo bottle, or even when you run a bath. His distress may lead to a tantrum. You can try to help him with his fears: for example, allow him to wash a doll's hair, or shampoo your hair and pour water over your own head, or distract him by letting him play with lots of bubbles in the bath as you shampoo.

Your toddler still needs lots of help and comfort, but he is becoming more independent and will want to complete a task, such as feeding himself: 'Me do it!'. He needs to feel that he is safe and secure in order to become more independent and explore the world for himself. For example, he may look to check where you are in playgroup. You will also see that he uses trial and error to solve a problem. When playing with a shape-sorter toy, he knows that shapes go through holes, but he may not know which one fits where, so he will try the holes in turn, or turn the shape different ways to try to make it fit.

How to help

- Use songs or rhymes that identify body parts. For example 'This little piggy', 'Heads, shoulders, knees and toes', 'This is the way we touch our knees, touch our knees, touch our knees' (to the tune of 'Here we go round the mulberry bush'), or the 'Hokey-cokey'.
- Let him point to the body parts on a doll or a stuffed toy, or on you and on himself. Once he is secure in knowing where his tummy is, he will find it hilarious if you get it wrong and touch his arm telling him it is his tummy.
- Encourage role play and make-believe by playing simple games, like making teddy a cup of tea or cleaning teddy's face.
- Count steps or other objects so that he begins to learn about the concept of numbers. As yet he may not know what the number 'one' or 'five' means but he may learn the rhythm of counting.

Should I worry? Is my child developing correctly?

See your doctor when your toddler is 2 years old if:

- he uses fewer than ten words
- he does not begin to link two words together (for example, 'want drink')
- he does not copy words or actions
- he does not know what to do with everyday objects (for example, a toothbrush or fork)
- he does not walk confidently
- he does not make a lot of eye contact
- he does not respond when he is called by his name.

You should also see your doctor if he loses a skill that he has previously mastered.

7

24–30 months

Mobility

From now on it can get difficult to keep up! Your child is now a confident walker and, if he has not already done so, starts to run. He is learning to walk backwards and sideways as well as forwards. He can walk on his feet or on his tip-toes and can get up from sitting to standing without help. When standing he can bend down to pick up something from the floor, or squat to play on the floor. He is strong enough to carry an object and walk, or drag or push something along with him. At around 2 years old your child learns to jump; initially you will see him do a sort of bunny hop or gallop as he lifts one leg in the air and then brings the other one up, before he learns to bend his knees and jump with both feet at the same time. When holding on, he can stand on one leg, which will help with his climbing skills, although he will not be able to balance on one leg without support for some time yet. He uses all his different gross motor skills to crawl, roll, walk, jump, climb and run, so he will be able to climb some steps onto the apparatus at the park, crawl through a tunnel, pick his way carefully over a balance beam (while holding on) and then slide down the slide to finish.

Do not worry if your child seems to fall over a lot when running: it is quite normal for him to trip and fall as he learns this skill. If you feel that he is falling more than is usual for him, it may be worth checking that his shoes fit properly; but if you feel that he is falling much more than other children, it may be worth visiting your doctor. It is normal for your child to look bow-legged at this age; however, if it is asymmetrical in that only one leg is bowed, or if he has, or develops, a limp – see your doctor (see also page 53).

Your child's stair-climbing skills are continuing to improve and he will learn to walk upstairs with alternate feet on alternate stairs, using one hand to hold your hand or the banister. If there are only a few stairs he may attempt to climb them without holding on to anything but he is more likely to rely on the banister, or if there is no banister, he may put his hands down on the step above him to help balance as he clambers up. Going up is easier than coming down and he is not yet likely to be able to climb down using alternate feet on alternate steps. Instead, he holds on to your hand or the banister and brings both feet down to each step before attempting the next. On his own, he may feel safer to crawl down or bump down the stairs on his bottom. His climbing skills are such that he can clamber up onto a chair without needing help.

At this age, your child is able to push himself along on a ride-on toy and ride a sturdy tricycle. He is able to actively kick a ball, as opposed to kicking it by running into it, and understands the concept of running after a ball and then kicking it again. He can also throw, though without much accuracy, using an overarm throw; but he can throw (or perhaps more accurately, forcefully drop) things into a basket or bin when standing close by. Catching is more difficult than throwing and although he may understand to hold his arms out in front of him in order to catch a ball, he cannot actually catch it; however, he can scoop up a ball which is rolled to him.

How to help

- Get out and about! When you are out, let him out of the buggy; there are low front walls to climb on (holding hands), paving stones to jump between, and puddles to jump and splash in.
- Find your local park and let him discover and clamber all over the apparatus. He loves to be adventurous and climb up high, or spin fast on a roundabout. It is natural to be concerned for his safety, for example when he has climbed the ladder to the slide for the first time, and reasonable to stand behind him to protect

him from falling, but do encourage his independence and give
him lots of praise for his achievements.
- Make walking a game. If he does not want to walk and is asking
repeatedly for the buggy, you could pretend to chase him down
the street, have races to the next tree or postbox, count the
manhole covers, pick a leaf from each tree as you go by or play
spot the red car.

Handling skills

Your child's handling skills will continue to develop: he can now use his
hands in a twisting motion, twisting his wrist to take the lid off a jar or
turn a doorknob, and using his thumb and forefinger to twist the top
of a tube, such as toothpaste. He will be able to build a tower of six to
eight blocks, though the enjoyment is still likely to be in knocking them
back over again!

Making marks on paper (colouring and scribbling) is often a favourite
pastime for children. Around this time you will notice that with practice
his marks will begin to change; now the scribbles turn into vertical and
horizontal lines as well as circular scribbles. He uses the different parts
of his hands for different skills; he will finger paint by dipping his whole
hand in the paint and stamping his hand on the page to make hand
prints, as well as using one finger to make marks. He will learn to fold a
piece of paper in half. His pincer grip continues to improve and he may
be able to pick up large beads to string on a thread.

Although some children remain ambidextrous until approximately
4 or 5 years old, you may begin to see your child's handedness at this
time. Handedness is not developed all at once (he will not wake up one
morning and suddenly favour his right or left hand), rather it evolves
over time, so you will gradually notice a pattern of when he uses one
hand rather than the other for a particular task. As this is developing
he may continue to switch between his hands, even during the same
task, so he may transfer a crayon between his hands and thus use both
hands for colouring. It is important that you do not favour one hand or
the other, but let your child discover his own hand dominance.

How to help

- Use playdough, which is great for exploring through play: cut out shapes, draw with a plastic fork, show him how to roll a sausage or ball, or pinch small pieces from a larger piece.
- Make some jewellery. Both girls and boys will enjoy this, and it helps to develop handling skills. Start by stringing empty cotton reels (they have a nice big central hole, but also other surrounding holes in case you miss) onto an old shoe lace, and progress to large beads.
- Practise the large arm and hand motions needed for writing. For example, build up arm strength by using a paintbrush or a roller to paint your fence with water, or make wide, sweeping circles in sand.
- Encourage mark making with crayons, pencils and pens. Paint with fingers, hands, brushes, rollers or sponges.

Speech and language

Receptive and expressive language continues to develop, meaning that your child understands more of what you say (receptive language) and says more that you understand (expressive language). By now he will have more words than you can count (by 30 months old he knows on average approximately 200 to 500 words), and you will understand the majority of what he says. He will be linking words together to make two- and three-word sentences and he begins to understand and use some basic grammar; for example, using plurals ('dog' to 'dogs') and tenses (though he may make some incorrect assumptions, such as 'I goed park' instead of 'I went'). As with pronunciation, it is not necessary to tell him he was wrong or he made a mistake; instead, simply repeat with the correct phrase 'Yes, you went to the park' and with time he will copy! He will call himself by his own name and will use 'I', 'me' and 'mine', although he is still likely to confuse them with 'you' and 'yours'. He uses questions such as 'what' or 'who' and can answer such questions as 'Who has come home?'.

Your child continues to understand many more words than he can say, and he can follow two-stage instructions, such as 'Go to the bedroom and get your shoes' (though he may not always choose to follow them!). He still uses non-verbal communication and picks up on non-verbal cues from your facial expression or tone of voice. This will continue: after all, we still pick up on non-verbal communication as adults.

If you have a bilingual household you may notice that your child's speech appears to be developing at a slightly slower rate than his friends. However, this is not a cause for concern because this delay is temporary: by 5 years old there is generally no difference in language skills, even though your child has two languages! It is also normal for your bilingual child to mix up both languages in the same phrase as he sorts out which words belong to which language. When another language is spoken at home or by one parent, you may be concerned that your child has a particular accent when speaking English, but his accent and pronunciation will continue to develop as he is exposed to multiple accents at nursery, school and from friends.

How to help
- Look at photos or pictures and ask him questions about who is in the picture, what they are feeling and what they are doing.
- Play games to show him the range of his voice; for example, copying shouting or whispering.
- Ask questions to keep up the conversation during play. For example, ask who he is making a cup of tea for.
- Encourage games that increase his vocabulary, such as a pointing game. For example, where is the tree, cloud, bush, mud, puddle ...?
- Keep singing and reading!

Social and emotional development

You will notice that getting your child dressed and undressed becomes much easier as he continues to learn to help you with the process. He may be able to undo a zip and once the zip is undone, or if you undo any buttons, he will be able to take off his coat or a shirt. When you undo his shoes he is able to pull them off his feet. If you start the process, he can help you to pull down his trousers, and then step out of them, or sit down to pull them off his ankles. The same applies for pants (if he is wearing them). Taking things off is easier than putting things on, so he will not as yet be able to do the reverse process, and put on his coat or shoes. However, if you pull a T-shirt over his head he is able to find the holes to put his arms in. At this age he is becoming more independent while still needing help, so you may see him switch between the two easily and quickly; from 'Me do it' to 'Mummy help me'.

Your child continues to develop his skills at mealtimes. He is using a spoon and a fork and is able to choose correctly whether it is more appropriate to use a spoon or his fingers. He is getting neater at eating, with less mess around his face and on the floor, as his hand to mouth coordination improves and he chews with his mouth shut. He can drink using a cup and tends to use two hands to steady the cup. He can also use a straw, and he is beginning to show the different actions required for different foods: to chew a cracker but to lick an ice cream!

From 2 years old your child may be ready to start potty training. Some signs that he may be ready include: he tells you if he is wet or dirty; his nappy is dry for a period of approximately 2 hours at a time, or after his nap; and/or he is interested in the concept (following you into the toilet and being aware of what you are doing, or role playing sitting on a potty). Your child may be ready for potty training earlier than 2 years old or may not be ready for a while yet. Even if he is dry in the day, he may not be dry at night for some time.

Your child may enjoy the comfort of a routine and you may find that he is pretty determined to stick to the same routine time after time. This can be in large terms, such as always brushing his teeth before he goes downstairs for breakfast, or in smaller terms, such as lining up his toy cars in a particular order. He is improving at playing by himself and will initiate or start an activity on his own, or will tell you what it is he wants to play. He begins to have an understanding about an increasing number of relationships, where he is in the family, who are 'Mummy', 'Daddy', his siblings and grandparents. Although he does not yet understand about what it means to be a girl or a boy and the differences between the two, he does know that he is a boy (or she a girl) and becomes aware that 'Mummy is a girl' and 'Daddy is a boy'.

While he continues to play alongside other children, you may find that your child starts to watch other children very carefully and may start to play with them in simple games such as chase. Sharing is definitely still a challenge, as is waiting for his turn, or waiting for anything, including your attention. He simply wants what he wants when he wants it and does not as yet have a concept of time as regards waiting. You should try to be clear about how long your child has to wait in a practical way that he can understand. For example, instead of 'Mummy will play in a minute' (how long is a minute, and do you actually mean 60 seconds or do you just mean 'later'?), try saying 'Mummy will play after I have put the shopping away'. This way, he will see the progress you are making and you can help him to wait by showing him that you have emptied three shopping bags and have one more to go. Involving him in the task will also make his wait easier. As time progresses he will be able to wait for longer periods.

Controlling his impulses is difficult for your child. He may understand that you want him to do something, but he cannot suppress his desire to do what he wants to do and he cannot reason that he could do it later. He may appear defiant, often saying 'no', and temper tantrums are common as he cannot fully understand his emotions and cannot manage his feelings. A tantrum may be the result of frustration and anger, and also of sadness or guilt (for example, if you told him off for doing something he knew he should not have done). He is learning to rein in his feelings but it is very easy for them to burst out of him. He can get distressed and frightened by his own tantrums because he simply does not yet know what to do with himself. Physical comfort in the form of a cuddle as well as lots of reassurance about what he is feeling may be helpful. Despite his impulses and tantrums, he is generally still very eager to please you and help out!

How to help
- Let him help with dressing and undressing. You can also make this into role play with a doll or stuffed toy, with him helping to dress his toy.
- Talk about the potty or toilet, and talk through the routine of the toilet, such as wiping, flushing and washing hands so that he will have an idea of what there is to learn.
- Play games that deal with the concept of time, such as counting the number of steps before the postbox, or counting to ten

before playing a game or waiting for 'Ready, steady, go' before starting to run.
- Encourage his play with other children. This can simply be interacting with other children in the library or park.
- Give plenty of cuddles!

Problem solving

Concentration and attention span are increasing for your child, and you will notice that he is able to spend more time playing with things he enjoys. However, he will also show you if he is not interested in something and will not play with it for long. He continues to solve problems by trial and error: for example, if a puzzle piece does not fit, he will either try it somewhere else or put it down to try another piece. This also applies to new objects, so you may see him pick something up, examine it carefully and then see if it does what he expects it to do. For example, if it is shaped like a pen he may try to draw but if this does not work he may look for a lid, or turn it over to find the part that writes. Your toddler will continue to observe you closely to give him clues as to what things do. He will copy your behaviour, which you can see when he practises making tea or washing up. He may also start to take on different roles, for example pretend to be an animal on his hands and knees. Your child is extremely creative and enjoys make-believe play, such as zooming around a toy car.

Memory is improving and so your child can recall events that happened (albeit recently) in the past: he will be able to tell you about his morning. He is also starting to understand about the concept of the future, but does not yet have a clear understanding of time, so if you tell him that you are going to the zoo tomorrow, he knows that it is going to happen but is not sure when (and may think that tomorrow is happening sooner than it is!). You should try to use well-known points of reference to help him to learn about time by saying 'We'll go to the park after your nap', rather than saying 'We'll go to the park later'.

Your child is continuing to learn about shapes and colours and also that objects are of different sizes, though he may not have the vocabulary to describe this. He is learning more parts of his own body and will happily point them out either on himself or on you. Since your child learns by exploring, he is extremely inquisitive, but he also has little sense of danger. You can warn him of danger but he does not yet know what danger actually means. Although he is more independent, he still needs supervision and safe places to play because his natural curiosity and lack of safety awareness can be a dangerous combination! This does not mean that he should not be allowed to explore new experiences, but you as his parent must strike a balance between his burgeoning independence, his sense of adventure and the need to keep him safe.

How to help

- Allow for quiet time and rest. The world is an exciting and stimulating place full of new sights, sounds, feelings and ideas. He finds it both thrilling and overwhelming and he needs time to assimilate all the information he has had to process that day. So it is important that he relaxes with you, perhaps reading a book or sitting close and quietly talking. At this age, he may drop his afternoon nap, so he also needs a physical rest.
- Give him time. He needs time to work out a problem or to work out what an object is and what it does. Even though he gets frustrated easily and some help will be needed, do not automatically correct him or tell him all the answers (for example, where a puzzle piece fits). Encourage role play and creative games. Get down on your hands and knees with him; swing your arm like an elephant trunk, stomp around as a rhino, and whoop and gibber like a monkey!
- Play matching games such as matching up coloured socks when doing the laundry to teach him about colour.

Should I worry? Is my child developing correctly?

See your doctor when your child is 30 months old if:

- he is not running or jumping
- he cannot climb the stairs
- he avoids eye contact
- he does not interact with other children or acknowledge their existence (but is in his 'own world')
- he does not role play or make believe
- he does not scribble
- he cannot make himself understood to strangers when talking
- he is not linking words together to form short sentences.

You should also see your doctor if he loses a skill that he has previously mastered.

30–36 months

Mobility

Your child continues to develop his gross motor system; walking, running, crawling and jumping. You may notice that his gait begins to change from a bow-legged (or cowboy style) gait into being more straight-legged, but at about 3 years old he may develop a knock-kneed gait (see page 81). As his skills improve you will notice that he stops walking or running into obstacles in his path and will be able to swerve to avoid them or run around them.

By 3 years old your child can walk on tip-toes. His jumping skills improve and he can now jump from a standing position with both feet in the air at the same time. When holding hands he may be able to stand on one leg for a short period of time. He is able to ride both ride-on toys and a sturdy tricycle, and may start to use a balance bike. He is also able to walk, or even run, while holding an object such as a toy or book, but is unlikely to be able to climb the stairs while holding an object, especially if you are not holding on to his other hand.

Stair-climbing skills are growing: he can now walk up the stairs using alternate feet on alternate stairs, though he is likely to prefer to hold on to your hand or the banister. If he is not holding on to something, you may notice that he still 'crawls' up the stairs (by putting his hands a few steps above the one he is on), or he may go back to bringing both feet up to the same step before continuing up. Going down is more difficult than climbing up: your child is still likely to be climbing down steps bringing both feet to the same step before attempting the next one, unless he is holding your hand, in which case he may attempt to use alternate feet on alternate stairs. He will be able to climb up a small ladder such as for a slide, and go down the slide on his own.

Ball skills are improving: by 3 years old he will run and actively kick a ball forwards, as opposed to kicking it by simply running into it. Throwing and catching still need a lot of practice! By now he can throw a ball in an overarm manner but without much accuracy. He is able to drop objects into a bag or bin and this gradually changes from being a dropping motion to a throwing motion. When sitting on the floor, he is accurate at rolling a ball back and forth between outstretched legs. He will also begin to catch a large ball or balloon when gently (and quite precisely!) thrown towards him.

How to help

- Play ball or balloon games, such as catch, rolling the ball or balloon football (kick the balloon into a laundry basket, box or bin to score a goal).
- Try jumping games. Trampolines are great but you can practise jumping without one. You could draw a square in chalk on the pavement and jump in and out of it, or you could jump over a cloth or piece of string on the floor which represents a river.
- Put on some music and dance together! Try copying each other spinning, jumping, marching around the table, clapping, flying round the room like an aeroplane with your arms stretched wide, or try dancing like different animals – use your arm as a trunk, jump like a kangaroo or stamp like a rhino!

Handling skills

By 3 years old your child is probably showing his 'handedness'; you can see if he is right- or left-handed. As handedness develops you will see that he begins to consistently use one hand or the other in most activities, such as painting or picking up a spoon.

As the pincer grip and fine motor skills develop you will notice that he can turn the pages of a paper book one at a time (prior to this he could only turn thick board book pages one at a time). His needle skills also improve and he can now hold a string or lace in one hand and use his pincer grip to string on three or four large wooden or plastic beads. He may be able to thread a lace in and out of lacing cards, putting the lace into the relevant hole, although he needs help with this because he does not yet know if the lace needs to go into the hole from above or below. His ability to build with bricks also continues to develop and he can build a tower of approximately eight bricks. He may even be able to copy a simple structure, such as a tunnel made with three blocks, or be able to use connecting bricks to build towers or other structures.

Play is also more sophisticated with playdough or other modelling clay. Prior to this age, he may have simply enjoyed the feel of the dough, squishing it in his hands; but now he starts to copy you in actions such as rolling the dough into a sausage or cylinder shape, rolling it into a ball (perhaps not particularly round at first), using a cutter to create a shape, or pulling and squeezing portions of dough from a bigger ball. Your child loves to paint and draw: he can use his hand and wrist to move the paintbrush in his hand. He can also paint with a roller or a sponge and will understand the process of dipping the tool into the paint before applying it to the paper. He holds a brush or crayon, using a pincer grip, between the thumb and fingers (not the whole fist) and he can copy vertical and horizontal strokes as well as circular motions. Try drawing a circle on a page and asking him to copy it; his attempt may not be perfectly round or may not join up very well, but by 3 years old it is likely to be generally circular.

How to help

- Get crafty, and do not worry about whether the end result looks professional and neat because it is the process of making the art that matters. Paints, felt-tip pens, crayons, chalks, sponge painting, vegetable printing, painting with water, sticking and gluing, sprinkling glitter from a shaker, sticking pieces of pasta on paper – the possibilities are endless! Be excited and proud of the end result and be sure to talk about it with him.

- Use playdough. You can make this yourself cheaply (see the Appendix), and can involve him in the making process (for example, stirring the mixture). Once made, show him how to roll sausages or balls. You could give him a plastic knife to practise cutting skills or use a cocktail stick to poke holes or draw on a rolled-out piece of playdough.
- Encourage playing with puzzles. Building with bricks and playing with shape-sorter toys improve his fine motor skills. Try using kitchen tongs to pick up building blocks or socks and put them in a box to develop his hand strength.

Speech and language

By the time he is 3 years old, your child is chatting away and you will be able to understand the vast majority of what he says: you can now have a conversation together. His speech is clear enough that he will be understood by strangers as well as his closest carers. He may talk to his teddy or dolls, chatting and asking them questions, but he is unlikely to play the role of the teddy, so you will not hear both sides of the conversation. He has a vocabulary of approximately 500 words and will be making sentences of at least three or four words. He can now identify different parts of his body and name various animals, foods, forms of transport and most familiar objects and people.

Grammar is also improving. For example, your child starts to understand that he can make plurals by adding an 's' to the end of words such as 'toy'/'toys', but he may also apply this rule incorrectly, such as 'I want two toasts' rather than 'I want two pieces of toast'. He is beginning to understand the concept of time, in that things happened in the past and will happen in the future, so he starts to use words such as 'tomorrow' or 'yesterday' (though these can be used indiscriminately to mean any time in the future and any time in the past, respectively). He links nouns and verbs together to make sentences such as 'Later read book' but he is unlikely to be aware of verb tenses, so will use the present tense to describe things in the future, present and past. As his sense of self (as a separate being to others) continues to develop, your child learns to refer to himself as 'me' or 'I' and not just by his own name. He will also start to use 'my' and 'mine', as opposed to 'you' and 'yours', correctly; so he now says 'pick me up' instead of 'pick you up'. Although he still gets confused and may say 'let I' instead of 'let me'. He can now understand prepositions, such as 'in' or 'under', and so is able to follow an instruction such as 'Please pick up the carrot from under the table'.

Your child now has a definite concept of questions and answers. He can use and answer questions such as 'Where is my …?', as well as questions relating to his name and age. He can hold a simple conversation with other children. As his language continues to develop, he can put his feelings into words and is better able to solve problems, though he still gets easily frustrated.

How to help

- Keep reading. He loves to hear the same stories over and over again: leave gaps as you read, which encourages him to fill in the spaces. Ask questions, discuss the pictures and keep talking!
- Sing songs with actions to help him to learn body parts, animals or particular movements.
- Get things wrong to make him laugh. For example, when handing him his breakfast toast say 'Here is your pasta' and watch his reaction; he will find it funny and also correct you, saying 'No, toast!'

Social and emotional development

Your 3-year-old child is not able to fully dress and undress himself without assistance, but he can do more for himself. He can pull down elasticated trousers (or skirt) and pants and take them off; he can undo Velcro™ straps and take off shoes; and he can open zips (and may have enough finger dexterity to be able to undo large buttons) and then take off his coat or shirt. Dressing is more difficult than undressing but he may try to put on his shoes (by closing Velcro™ straps, not by tying up shoelaces). He will help you by stepping into the leg holes of his underwear or trousers and may start to try to pull them up. He continues to put his arms into the arm holes of his tops, but is not yet able to put on or take off a jumper or T-shirt by himself.

By this age, your child may be toilet trained in the day but probably not at night. If he is interested in the potty or toilet, is dry for at least 2 hours at a time, or tells you when he has done a wee or a poo, he is ready for potty training. Once he understands the concept of the toilet, his language skills are now developed enough for him to be able to tell you when he needs to go. Remember to give lots of encouragement and praise when he does manage to use the potty or toilet. No matter how or when you tackle potty training, be prepared with lots of spare underwear for the inevitable accidents!

You may find that your child becomes increasingly interested in cooking and preparing food so it is a good opportunity to start simple cooking with him. Although he may not yet be able to weigh or measure, he can pour and mix! He may be able to wash his hands at this age, though he may still need help. With encouragement, he can lay cutlery on the table and take his empty plate to the sink after eating. He is not yet able to cut up his food but he can use a spoon with increasing neatness and can stab foods with a fork and then transfer them to his mouth.

Although he is interested and excited by new experiences, your child still enjoys the structure of routine. If there is a big change to the routine, such as moving house, you may find that he needs extra reassurance. However, he is becoming more adept at adapting to new situations and you may notice that he is beginning to have less separation anxiety when going to new places such as nursery or playgroup. As he becomes progressively independent, you will notice that although he still plays alongside other children, he is increasingly able to play with them and take turns in games. For this reason, playgroup begins to feel more relaxed. He is able to experience and vocalise a wide range of emotions, such as happiness, sadness, fear, shame and guilt; and he is able to sympathise and show concern when a friend is distressed. This marks a change from his earlier self, when he was unable to separate his emotions from yours and he became upset when you were upset. He now becomes concerned that you are upset, wants to find out why this is, and offer you comfort. However, as before, it is easy for any emotion to become overwhelming and then he becomes upset.

As your child becomes better able to identify his emotions, there will (hopefully) be fewer tantrums. Yet there is still a battle between his will and yours: he may not stop an activity when you ask him to because he still struggles to understand why he should! When overwhelmed, he is still likely to hit out, or snatch toys from others, but he is more able to deal with his feelings. Keep talking to him and explain your reasoning. It is also helpful to pick your battles: instead of asking him to stop the puzzle and get dressed, ask him to come and get dressed when he has finished. Sharing continues to be difficult, but he is beginning to comprehend that not everything belongs to him, so he may understand 'mine' versus 'his', 'hers' or 'theirs'. He is extremely affectionate and shows real love for his friends and family, being pleased to see them and giving cuddles and smiles. His sense of self continues to develop and he will be able to point to himself and to other people in photographs.

How to help

- Practise cutlery skills using playdough; he can stab pieces with a fork and cut it up with a plastic knife.
- Encourage role play with soft toys. You can role play mealtimes, bath times and getting dressed and undressed to practise all these situations.
- Give as many cuddles and as much physical contact as he needs.
- Keep calm when he is distressed and talk calmly about a situation. It may be useful to read books about new situations, such as going to the dentist or nursery.
- Play games that encourage turn taking, even simple games such as taking turns to kick a ball or to match shapes or colours.
- Let him make some simple decisions. This helps him to feel that he has some control over a situation: for example, if putting his pants on is a battle, let him pick the colour of the pants.

Problem solving

You will notice that your child's concentration and attention span continue to increase and he is able to play on his own for longer periods of time. As with all of us, no matter what age, we will concentrate for longer periods at things which interest us, so if your child is interested in something it is not unusual for him to want to play it for long periods of time, or to play it repeatedly. He can work increasingly complicated toys, using handles, switches, levers, buttons and other moving parts and will be able to investigate these on his own without necessarily being shown them first. He can connect linking blocks together and will use the skills he learnt on one object for use on another, for example twisting a doorknob and untwisting a jar, or if he has one toy where the red button makes a noise he will try the red button on another toy to see if it does the same thing. At this age he will be able to do simple puzzles of four to six pieces on his own and to complete harder puzzles with help.

Your child is beginning to have a sense of numbers and understands what two, or even three, is and will be able to tell you when he has two things left. He may even begin to recognise the first letter of his own name. He may also further develop his idea of time, being aware that bath time comes after dinner time and will be able to tell you that it is bath time.

How to help

- Encourage role play with different jobs, such as a builder or doctor. Not only will this encourage handling skills if you use the relevant toy objects, but also speech and the ability to empathise in different situations.
- Give him time to work things out on his own. The urge to help can be powerful, but unless he is getting frustrated, let him try to work things out himself, be it a toy or puzzle or other situation.
- Keep counting – from the number of stairs he is climbing, to the number of cars until you find your own in the car park – and point out numbers on houses or other signs.
- Play colour and shape games to continue to reinforce this knowledge. Games involving matching colours can be useful for taking turns as well as for learning the vocabulary around colours.

Should I worry? Is my child developing correctly?

See your doctor when your child is 3 years old if:

- he is falling over continuously, or limping, or cannot climb stairs
- he does not understand simple instructions, such as 'Pick up your teddy'
- he does not speak clearly or cannot make himself understood
- he has very limited eye contact
- he is unable to play with simple toys, such as a two- to four-piece puzzle or shape-sorter toy
- he does not appear interested in other people or children
- he does not role play or make believe.

You should also see your doctor if he loses a skill that he has previously mastered.

3–4 years

Mobility

By now it can become difficult to keep up with your walking, running, climbing, jumping, dancing and spinning child; running after him all day is great for your physical fitness! He is becoming increasingly agile in travelling forwards and backwards. As your child becomes stronger in the core his balance improves and he becomes able to walk along a plank or beam (close to the floor!) with his arms spread out for balance.

At this age he may walk with his feet pointing inwards and may also have a knock-kneed gait, where there is a large gap between the lower legs when standing with the knees together. This is a normal variation and tends to resolve as the legs straighten by approximately 7 years old. However, if the extent of knock-knees is so severe that it is interfering with mobility, or if it affects one side only, then see your doctor.

Your child can now ride a push-along toy, pedal a tricycle and perhaps start to use a scooter and/or balance bike (which is a bike that does not have pedals; the child pushes himself along with his feet, aiming to balance with both feet off the floor, which teaches the balancing skills required to ride a conventional bike later on). As he becomes stronger, your child will be able to stand on one leg, initially holding your hands for support but then being able to stand for very short periods (only a few seconds) on one leg without support. By 4 years old some children may be able to hop. This ability to stand on one leg will also help with his stair-climbing skills and during this year he will be able to climb up and down the stairs without holding on, using alternate feet on alternate steps.

Ball skills continue to develop. Your child can roll a ball and scoop up a ball that is rolled to him. He is starting to throw more accurately, using both his shoulder and elbow to throw the ball. Catching a ball is more difficult and although he may understand the concept, he will not yet move his hands towards the ball to bring it in to his body. However, if the ball is gently thrown into his outstretched arms he will scoop it inwards to catch it. If you gently bounce a ball towards him you will notice that he starts to move towards the ball to catch it. He can now run towards a stationary ball and kick it forwards with increasing accuracy and strength, so the ball travels further.

Your child will need to be strong in order to be able to sit at school at a desk and write for long periods, so encourage lots of physical activity throughout the day: running around playing counts as physical activity!

How to help

- Use your local park, low front walls or local children's centres to improve his strength, agility and balancing skills. Practise ball games, perhaps make it into a game using another skill, such as counting (for example, 'Can we throw the ball to each other ten times?').
- Encourage him to ride a tricycle or scooter outdoors, but be sure to reinforce road safety rules. Make sure he wears a helmet and discuss staying on the pavement, watching for cars coming out of driveways, not going too far ahead and stopping when you call 'Stop!'.
- Be sure to give him some quieter activities so that he can rest and reboot! Although it seems like he has a limitless reserve of energy, he will find it difficult to pace himself or tell you he is tired if there are lots of exciting things to do.

Handling skills

At this age, your child is likely to have developed his handedness and will consistently use one hand in preference to the other for skilled handling tasks. As his manual dexterity improves you will notice that his drawing and writing skills continue to develop and he will progress from circular and linear scribbles to being able to draw square shapes. He will start to draw figures with body parts; initially these are generally faces but then more body parts are added on. By 4 years old he can draw figures with two to four body parts, for example a head with two arms sticking out of it. By this age, he may be able to hold a pencil correctly (but he may not yet have the hand strength to do so). He may even begin to be able to draw some capital letters, often the more linear letters such as H or E. His brick-building skills will also develop and he can balance and build increasingly large towers of bricks and copy a tunnel made of three bricks. He can also cut with scissors, which is a difficult skill requiring coordination and strength of the thumb and forefinger in one hand while holding the piece of paper with the other. Be sure that your child is using child-safe round-ended scissors!

How to help

- Give plenty of opportunities to build arm and hand strength and practise the motions which will be required for writing later on. For example, let him write in sand or shaving foam using big arm motions or, if it is muddy out, then let him get a stick and make patterns in the mud (or forget the stick and let him get down and dirty in the muck!).
- Continue to use playdough to develop manual dexterity: practise rolling, making balls or sausage shapes, cutting, pinching and squeezing the dough.
- Encourage hand strength using child chopsticks (these are joined together at the top) or a pair of large child's tweezers to pick up objects. Try transferring raisins from one container to another; perhaps if he can manage to transfer and count to ten (with help) he gets to eat them!
- Beads and sewing are also great to develop hand strength.

Speech and language

Talking more and more, your child now knows over 1,000 words and is linking them together in simple sentences of increasing length (approximately 5 or 6 words). You may notice that he is stumbling or stuttering over words as he tries to get words out quicker than he can physically say them. At this age, a stammer or stutter is part of normal language development and no cause for concern: he simply has so much to say that he cannot always get it out! By now even strangers will be able to understand the majority of your child's speech (though some children will be speaking more clearly than others).

Your child has now acquired a basic understanding of grammar. For example he knows that in English an adjective goes before a noun 'This is a red book' or 'The book is red' and not 'This is a book red' or 'The red is book'. He will use question words correctly and understand 'where', 'what', 'who' and 'why'. The concept of 'when' is more difficult because it is linked to an understanding of the concept of time, though this is also developing and he is able to talk about things that happened this morning or yesterday and can tell you if something is happening tomorrow. However, everything in the future may be referred to as 'tomorrow', and everything in the past, no matter how long ago, may be referred to as 'yesterday'. He also understands and uses prepositions such as 'over' and 'under'; and he knows the difference between 'you' and 'me'.

Children love reading books and stories, often the same story over and over (and over) again, and your child will get cross if you miss a page, line or even a word. At around this age he begins to join in with well-known stories and can fill in well-known lines, for example 'I'll huff and I'll puff and I'll blow your house down' from *The Three Little Pigs*. He is then able to tell you what will happen next in a story that he knows well, and progresses to being able to recount or repeat the whole story. He can also give you a report of what happened to him during the course of the day, but may need signposting with time-related questions, such as 'what did you do after breakfast?'

How to help

- Give him time to talk. If he appears to be stuttering over a word, do not fill it in for him but give him the time to come out with the sentence himself.

- Try not to correct inaccurate grammar or pronunciation of new words; instead, repeat the phrase correctly to give him an opportunity to hear the correct phrasing.
- Be patient and try to answer the many, many questions that he may have. Not only does this increase his language skills by introducing him to new words, but it also develops his problem-solving skills as he continues to develop an understanding of the world. However, if the constant questions become too much then you can say that you need some quiet time for a few minutes as this momentary respite may allow you to return to answering questions with enthusiasm!
- Encourage an imaginary world of play by telling stories and reading books, which helps to develop creativity, an ability to understand others and language skills.

Social and emotional development

Your child is becoming more independent with regards to dressing and undressing himself. Undressing is easier than dressing and your child has already mastered the ability to pull down his underpants and trousers and take off his socks. In this year he will gradually be able to unbutton large buttons, unzip zips and unbuckle a belt, and may begin to pull off T-shirts and jumpers. With regards to dressing, he begins to be able to put on his socks and shoes (with Velcro™ fasteners) – though he may well put his shoes on the wrong feet. He will be able to identify which side of his clothing is the front, so if you help him to pull a pullover over his head he will twist it around so that the front faces the front before putting his arms through the arm holes (though he may still need help with this). He will be able to pull up underpants and trousers and will be able to button large buttons (though the smaller buttons on trousers, skirts and shirts will still be difficult, as will pulling on a pair of tights). By 4 years old he may be able to put a zip together at the base before pulling it shut. He will be able to brush his teeth, though will still need help to ensure that they are properly cleaned.

By now your child has mastered a fork and spoon and he will continue to get neater and more efficient when eating. He is unlikely as yet to be able to use a knife effectively and may use his fingers to help push food onto a fork or spoon. He is drinking from a glass and can use a straw. However, you may find that he is getting increasingly fussy or is asking for treats more and more often. Try not to let meals turn into a battlefield, difficult as it can be; instead, focus on praising him for eating or trying new foods and avoid criticising him for not doing so. Encourage mealtimes as a family social affair where you talk about your day and spend time as a family.

If your child is not already toilet trained, he is likely to be ready this year. Even if he is dry in the day, he may not yet be ready to be dry at night. He may be ready to be toilet trained at night if his nappy is dry or only very slightly wet in the morning consistently for a few nights, or if he wakes up telling you that he needs to go to the toilet. Even if he is dry in the day or night, accidents are still common.

You may notice that the tantrums of the 'terrible twos' begin to decrease as your child begins to be able to control his strong emotions and feelings and also as his language skills develop enough for him to be able to tell you what he is feeling. Even though he may still have tantrums or crying fits, these may not be as violent as before – there may be less lying on the floor kicking and screaming, as he is getting control of himself.

At this age your child is really eager to please you and help you with tasks or jobs around the house; being a 'little helper'. He is also beginning to learn how to play with and get on with other children. He understands that people are separate beings from him and as such have their own feelings, so he may worry or show concern when another child is upset, but will be able to differentiate their feelings from his own. He is likely to role play, with games such as Mummies and Daddies to help him to develop his understanding of other people. His realisation that he is separate from you also means that he now understands that you do not always automatically know what he wants and needs, and so he has to ask! His sense of self continues to develop and he will learn how old he is and he will know his sex. (He can be quite preoccupied with who is a girl and who is a boy.)

Your child's ability to share and take turns is improving (in a small group; waiting too long for a turn is difficult). However, you may notice that he finds sharing easier at a playgroup than at home because he understands that the toys in playgroup are always for sharing but at home he may not have to share, so this can be difficult when a friend comes for a playdate. Even as his sharing abilities continue to develop he may not be able to share his most precious, or newest, toy. He may still be using his comfort blanket and is unlikely to be able to share that at all! His ability to wait also improves, but it is important to try to be clear about how long he has to wait. Saying 'in a minute' when you mean 10 minutes will be difficult for him, especially as he does not yet have an idea of the length of a minute. Instead, you should continue to signpost with activities that he does understand, for example, 'Yes, we can do that puzzle after we put away your cars'.

Sense of humour also continues to develop and your child will laugh at silly words, mispronunciations, funny faces and physical humour (such as you falling over when he pats you). You may also notice that he develops strong fears, such as fear of the dark or of monsters. Instead of telling him that there is nothing to worry about, you should acknowledge his fears and perhaps try giving him a tool to help him to deal with them. For example, you could say that there is nothing nasty hiding in the dark; that it is the same as the day but with the lights off. You can leave a night light in his bedroom and also a special teddy to be his nighttime protector and help look after him at night.

From 3 years old, children in the UK are entitled to 15 hours of free nursery education per week. This is not compulsory but many children will attend a nursery before formal school starts the following year. (For further information about helping your child at school, see Chapter 14.)

How to help

- Encourage independence at mealtimes and try not to worry about the mess!
- Continue role play. Try taking on different roles each time – doctors, mummies, firemen, animals, etc.
- Play simple turn-taking games at home so that he becomes used to the skill of waiting for his turn. For example, even something as basic as he puts away one block and then has to wait for you to put your block away before he does the next. Also play games that require cooperation, such as building a tower together.

Problem solving

The sometimes incessant questioning of the average 3-year-old (why, why, why?), no matter what answer you give, is a normal part of cognitive development. How can your child develop an understanding of the world unless he asks questions about it? So, although it can be frustrating, try to answer – and if you do not know, then say that too!

At this age your child has a well-developed imagination and can find it difficult to separate the inner world from the outer world (what is pretend or imaginary and what is real). After all, the animals in a book may be able to talk, or a teddy in a book may be able to walk and talk, so to your child, why should this not happen in real life? This sometimes leads to anxieties and fears: if the animals in the story came out of the book and came alive, it is reasonable that he may be scared of this happening in real life. Sometimes this means that he may tell you things which he has imagined as facts, because he may not yet be able to tell the difference. For example, if you ask him what he did today, he may seriously tell you that he 'went flying'; he is not lying, rather he is confused between what he played doing, pretended to do or simply wanted to do.

The blurred boundaries between the real and the imaginary may explain why your child may develop an imaginary friend. This friend can be based on a person, animal, object (such as a soft toy) or a magical creature. Do not worry if he is chatting away to his imaginary friend, or tells you about the friend. An imaginary friend does not mean that he is lonely or unhappy: rather, the experience is a common part of child development and may be a sign of great imagination and creativity. This friend exists for your child and is true to him. An imaginary friend provides friendship and companionship and a tool to try out imaginary games, stories and test the rules of friendship. The friend can also provide support for any anxieties, allow your child to be in charge (when normally he is not), potentially provide an outlet for naughtiness and may even give you some clues and insight into your child. For example, if his imaginary friend is afraid of dogs and so your child has to avoid them, it may be that he is afraid of dogs. Studies show that if you ask too many questions and get too involved, the imaginary friend may disappear, so it may be helpful to appear interested but not to be too overly keen for details. While it is reasonable to play along, perhaps setting another seat at the dinner table, it is important that the imaginary friend does not become too controlling. For example, if your child makes a mess and says that his imaginary friend did it so he should not clear up, it is important to emphasise that he still needs to help tidy; or if he does not want to go to bed because the imaginary friend does not have to, keep firm, saying something like 'You still have to go to bed; if Mark doesn't want to go he doesn't have to, or he can come too – up to him – but you still need to go to bed'. Do not worry if his imaginary friend is a constant presence for quite a long time: the friend tends to disappear as your child gets older, simply slipping quietly away.

In this year your child will develop a concept termed 'theory of mind', which is the idea that other people may not always be aware of the same information as him. For example, there is a famous experiment called the 'Sally-Anne experiment'. Children are shown marbles and a doll named Sally. Sally takes a marble and puts it in her basket before leaving the room. The children are then shown another doll, named Anne, who comes into the room, removes the marble from Sally's basket, puts it into her own box, and then leaves the room. Sally returns to the room and the children are asked where she would look for the marble. At younger than approximately 4 years old, children will indicate Anne's box because they do not yet realise that Sally was not aware of the change. Yet at 4 years old, children indicate that Sally will look in her own basket, showing that they understand that Sally does not have all the information about the situation. For your child, the theory of mind is essentially the understanding that other people know different things, and that not everyone knows what he is thinking.

Your child can now name the most common colours and shapes. He also begins to have an understanding of objects being the 'same' and 'different', so he can sort out objects according to colour and shape. For example, he can put all the red socks in one pile. He can complete puzzles of increasing difficulty, matching pieces by shape, by colour or more systematically by starting with the edges. His understanding of time continues to develop but is still quite general, such as morning and nighttime, or before and after lunch. He is developing an understanding of size, such as big and little. He knows the names and order of numbers for counting, and also understands 'one-to-one correspondence', which is the idea that when you count raisins, for example, you count each raisin as one object, that the number one is the first raisin you count, then number two and systematically onwards; he does not return to a raisin that he has already counted.

How to help

- Try sorting games. You can sort everything from laundry to toys, sorting by colour or shape.
- Encourage puzzles and other building games.
- Play along with his imaginary friend!
- Practise counting – counting forwards to ten and then back again. Count objects with him, for example, count fish fingers before putting them on the plate. Numbers are everywhere, from numbers on houses to prices in shops: point them out and use them (count the packets into the shopping trolley and count the bags out of the car).
- Develop his colour knowledge by playing simple games such as I Spy ('I spy with my little eye, something the colour green') or spotting particular colours of cars in a car park.

Should I worry? Is my child developing correctly?

See your doctor when your child is 4 years old if:

- he is unable to jump
- he does not make any scribbling marks on paper
- he cannot build a tower of three or four blocks
- he does not help at all with dressing
- he does not seem interested in other children
- he does not have eye contact
- he does not use simple sentences, or does not speak clearly enough to be understood
- he does not seem to understand what you say to him, such as a simple two- to three-stage command (for example, 'Please go into the kitchen and bring me your shoes')
- he does not use 'me' and 'you' correctly.

You should also see your doctor if he loses a skill that he has previously mastered.

10

4–5 years

Mobility

Your child will now be able to walk and run forwards and backwards, jump, gallop and climb and will be on the go constantly. As he continues to become stronger (and grow taller), he will be able to run faster and you will notice that his coordination continues to improve. As he runs he will be able to jump or leap over small objects, and swerve out of the way of larger objects. He will be able to stand on tip-toes and walk on both his tip-toes and his heels. He is now able to stand on one leg for longer periods of time, about 10 seconds or so, and will start to hop on one leg. Once he is able to hop on each leg, he may then learn how to skip along from one foot to the other (without a skipping rope). This ability to stand on one leg also means that he is able to walk up and down the stairs with increasing speed, using alternate feet on alternate stairs.

Balance continues to improve and your child will become more stable walking along a balance beam or walking on a straight line marked out on the floor, with his arms held out for balance and generally quite a lot of wobbling! With help, he may be able to do a forwards somersault. His ball skills also continue to improve: he is better able to kick with increasing accuracy and strength, throw and begin to catch a ball, and start to hit a ball with a bat. He can now scoot on a scooter and ride on a tricycle and on a balance bike. This skill, as with so many skills, is not just about the physical strength required to push himself along on the balance bike, but also the coordination required to steer and an ability to respond to external factors such as having to push harder to go up a hill, or understanding that he does not have to work so hard when going down a hill. At the same time as all of this, he still has to be aware of your instructions, for example if you call him to stop, and keep a look out for other people and obstacles!

How to help

- Walk to school if possible, and if not, get off the bus a stop early or park a 5 to 10 minute walk away. This walking is not only good for his physical health and fitness, but is also a great opportunity for time to talk together.
- Give plenty of opportunities to run around in the park, or garden if you have one. Local gymnastics or sports halls may have indoor soft play opportunities if the weather is poor. Although he is able to sit for longer periods of time, he still needs plenty of physical activity to encourage fitness and to help him to develop strength.
- Get the whole family moving: walking together, swimming, cycling – any activity!
- Consider a more structured class-led activity such as football or gymnastics. His school may provide after-school clubs, or find out what your local sports centre or children's centre offers.

Handling skills

Your child's dexterity and hand strength continues to develop. For example, at 5 years old he will be able to touch the pad of each finger to his thumb. During this year he will be able to build a tower of ten blocks and if it is demonstrated to him first, he will be able to build a flight of four steps from ten blocks (see Figure 5).

Writing and painting skills continue to improve. Your child can copy circles, squares, crosses and triangles and starts to draw a recognisable house (with windows, doors and a roof) and a person with four to six body parts. He starts to control his colouring and will begin to try to colour inside the lines of a picture. At school he may also be starting to learn to write letters. Initially the movements for making letters will be large, for example writing with a finger in sand or shaving foam.

Figure 5

Over time the size decreases, for example writing with a board pen on a small whiteboard and then, finally, using a pencil on paper. Writing letters not only involves being able to make your hand form the correct shape, but also requires him to apply enough pressure with the pencil in order to make the mark on the paper (but not too much so the paper rips). At this age he will start to write his own name. His skills using scissors will also improve; he can follow and cut along a straight line and may start to be able to follow a curved line, such as cutting out a large circular shape. Cutting out linear shapes that require turning a corner (such as a square or triangle) is more difficult and will not be mastered until he is older.

Although he cannot yet tie his shoe laces, your child can thread beads on a string, lace or sew sewing cards. He is more dextrous at using tools such as a screwdriver, or turning keys in a lock, and will become increasingly skilled at building with blocks and interlocking blocks of all sizes, from large wooden blocks to small bricks such as Lego™.

How to help

- Keep up physical activity to develop the core strength required to sit at a desk or table, hold a pencil and write: walking to school, playing in the park or indoors at soft play, or indeed any physical activity!
- Continue to encourage large movements of his arm such as painting a fence with water or using a stick to draw in sand or mud.
- Play with playdough. Some parents are concerned that playdough is only for younger children, but this is not the case; continuing to play with playdough encourages both handling skills and creativity.
- Build up hand strength by playing games with large tweezers, and increase hand dexterity with toys and crafts that have small parts, such as Hama™ beads, Rainbow Loom™ bands or Lego™.
- Let him help you to fix things around the house so that he practises using tools (under safe supervision).

Speech and language

During this year both his receptive language (what he understands) and expressive language (what he can say) will continue to improve. Your child's vocabulary is now about 1,000 to 2,000 words, but he understands far more words than he can say. As his vocabulary improves, so does his grammar and sentence structure and he will create longer sentences with a richer and more descriptive feel to better mirror what he means and sees. He links sentences together: for example, rather than saying 'There is the cat. Cat is brown', he says 'There is the brown cat' or 'There is the cat with brown fur'. He can use the past and future tenses, though he is still likely to make mistakes ('I drawed a picture'). He will still be asking plenty of 'why' questions as he tries to increase his understanding of the world.

Pronunciation of words also continues to improve and strangers will be able to understand your child when he speaks. He may still stumble or mispronounce long words, such as 'poppohitamus' for 'hippopotamus'. Some speech sounds may still be tricky, like 'th' and 'r'. For example, 'things' are often pronounced 'fings', 'three' as 'free' and 'rain' as 'wain'.

Your child is now able to use time words to sequence events as he tells them to you, such as 'before', 'after' and 'then'. He can recount a story, be it something that happened to him or a well-known book. He has a repertoire of nursery rhymes and other songs that he is able to sing. He is able to take turns during conversation, though this may still be difficult if he is really excited and desperate to tell you something! During conversation he can put his own view across and tell you his opinion or wants. His language skills have improved to the extent that he is able to understand idioms, for example 'It's raining cats and dogs' or 'He's a silly sausage', and knows that they are not to be taken literally.

How to help

- Keep talking! This sounds obvious and easy but actually takes time and patience. You may find that he is too tired to talk much on the way home from school when you ask him about his day (what he had for lunch, etc.). He may be more willing to engage in conversation over dinner or at bath time. Ask questions, but do not pester too much for information as this can make him pull back further!
- Play word games. For example: rhyming games such as you say a word and then he replies with a word that rhymes; taking turns to name opposites; or I Spy games ('I spy something starting with an 's' sound').
- Read, read, read! He may be learning to read at school and so has a reading book to take home for practice. Allowing him time to read to you is important but you should also keep reading stories to him as this gives plenty of opportunity for language development.

Social and emotional development

By 5 years old your child is likely to be able to dress and undress himself, only needing help with complicated fastenings, tiny or stiff buttons and tying his shoelaces. He can undo buttons and zips and take his clothes off, including pulling a jumper over his head; and he can get himself dressed, sorting out the front of clothes from the back and doing up buttons, zips and Velcro™. At school he may have to change for PE classes, and shoes that fasten with Velcro™ are easier than shoelaces. Changing for PE helps to consolidate his dressing and undressing skills.

Your child can brush his teeth, however he is unlikely to be able to brush them well until he is 7 or 8 years old so he will still need help with this task. He will be able to wash his hands, though getting them completely clean after he has got messy may also require a little help! At this age your child will be toilet trained in the daytime and may be completely independent in this: going to the toilet himself, pulling down his clothes, wiping himself, getting dressed again and washing his hands (although he may need reminding about flushing the chain or washing his hands). He may learn to become dry at night during this year or perhaps not yet. Signs that your child may be ready to forgo a nappy at night include him being dry, or only slightly damp, in the morning, or waking at night to go to the toilet. Bedwetting is common: you can help your child by taking him to the toilet just before bed and a waterproof sheet to go under the bottom sheet of his bed is also useful. Bedwetting is not considered to be a medical issue until he is more than 5 years old, at which age your doctor can advise you further.

At mealtimes, your child can use a fork and spoon accurately, making less mess as he eats. He will be able to spread a piece of bread or toast with butter, and may be able to start using a knife to cut foods.

Social skills continue to develop: your child makes friends at school, playing with them, as opposed to alongside them. He can take turns, is better able to share and also to work collaboratively with friends on a project or game. For example, 'Let's play mummies and daddies, I will be the daddy, you will be the mummy and you can be the baby'. He will show sympathy to a friend who is hurt or upset and may try to resolve conflict among his friends, for example suggesting that two people can play together. He also begins to understand that his friends may not have the same feelings as him; that although he wants to do something, his friend may not and that they may need to agree to both do something else together. He will want to please his friends and family and be helpful, though he may also be bossy! Although he will still need adult help with these interactions, you will notice that he will become increasingly able to deal with these situations on his own.

Your child has times when he is naughty, noisy, bossy, shows off or is just generally silly, and by now he has developed a sense of humour. He will push your patience to test what is acceptable behaviour because he needs to find out where these boundaries are in order to feel safe and confident about exploring the world. Despite understanding why he feels them, your child still finds it difficult to deal with certain emotions and feelings, and so he may develop some coping mechanisms. For example, if he feels overwhelmed at school, he may retreat to the quiet corner with a book, or quietly draw a picture, before returning to a more boisterous activity. He can now put his emotions into words and describe what he is feeling and why, although the emotions themselves still remain difficult to deal with. For example, instead of crying, he can explain to you that he is upset because his friend will not play with him, but he is still upset despite the lack of tears. You can help him by suggesting methods to deal with the emotion: for example, suggest that he plays with someone else, or something else, or explain that his friend is busy.

Role play continues to be a helpful tool for your child to try out other roles and characters in order to experience different situations and emotions. From everyday household chores to a visit to the doctor, role play can help him to make sense of the world and the relationships between different people within it. So when you take him for his pre-school booster jabs, you may see him playing at giving his teddy the vaccines in order to take control of the situation. He is becoming better able to distinguish reality from fantasy although this is still not fully established: he may still have an imaginary friend. You may notice that he tells you what he thinks you want to hear: for example, when you ask 'What did you have for lunch at school today?', he replies 'I had fish and potatoes and peas', even though he only ate the potatoes and dessert, because he knows that you want him to eat vegetables! He is not meaning to deceive you in a malicious way; rather, he wants to please you, so he tells you he has eaten his vegetables!

Since starting school, your child understands that you drop him off and pick him up again later, so he is better able to cope with your absence at other times. His sense of self continues to develop and he knows his sex, his name and his age. He may also identify himself by comparing himself to others he knows, for example 'I have a goldfish but Fred doesn't'. Despite your child becoming more and more independent, he is still in an age of transition, so there are times when he wants even more hugs and reassurances than before. He still wants to feel your support as he becomes independent, so although he wants to go off at a party to play with his friends on his own, he may come back to check that you are still around.

How to help

- Make sure that there is plenty of time for talking: at mealtimes, during the journey to and from school, bath time, etc.
- Give him opportunities to talk about his feelings.
- Listen to what he says when he talks. This sounds simple, but the urge to interrupt with a solution, suggestion or question is strong.
- Discuss his conflicts to help him to look at it from all perspectives. For example, 'How would you feel if Billy said that to you?'.
- Encourage role play. If you know that there is a potentially difficult situation coming up, then try to practise it in advance. For example, if you know that he gets upset at school when told by another child that he cannot join in, you could role play different solutions.
- Reading books or drawing pictures about specific social situations, like making a new friend at school, can help him to explore social skills and adapt to change.
- Be clear about acceptable and unacceptable behaviour – even though he now argues back, you are still in charge!

Problem solving

This is the year during which your child will start primary school, in the Reception class. In the UK, it is the first year of formal schooling. At this stage, much of the learning is carried out through play and role play but he will learn to recognise all his letters and numbers during the course of the year. He will also start to blend the letters together to begin the process of reading. For advice regarding starting school, and helping with literacy and numeracy, see Chapter 14.

When your child begins to write some letters and numbers, they may be enormous, back to front or in mirror writing. None of these are concerns because he is still developing strength in his arms and hands as well as a technical understanding of how to write. He will be able to recognise his own name written down, even before he can read. Your child can now count to at least ten and understands the concept of one-to-one correspondence, which means that when he is counting the number of objects in a group, he counts each object only once. (You may notice that he touches each object as he counts it.) Although he may be unable to count to large numbers such as those over twenty, he will be able to identify which group of objects has 'lots' or 'more' and may begin to estimate how many there are in a group. He will also develop an understanding of what figures on the page mean, so if he sees the number 3 next to a picture of a teddy bear, he will understand that there are three teddy bears.

Your child can group objects according to different classifications; for example by size, colour or shape, and will be able to identify basic colours and shapes. He can order objects according to size: shortest to tallest or smallest to biggest and vice versa. He is learning the concept of opposites and also starts to be able to recognise and create rhyming words. He is now able to draw a person with at least six body parts, which looks increasingly like a person! Attention span and ability to concentrate continue to improve in your child. You may notice that he talks to himself as he plays alone: this is a method he uses to guide himself through what he is doing now and what to do next. He is developing an understanding about how the world works: for example, that you pay for items in a shop using money, or that a policeman is there to help you if you are lost. He may know his telephone number and/or his address. He is still learning by a combination of methods: through play, observation, plenty of questions and by trial and error!

How to help

- Play matching and sorting games; by size, shape, weight or colour, be it the family washing, pasta shapes or pictures on cards.
- Introduce memory games. For example, 'I went to the supermarket and bought', when you each add one item to the list as you go back and forth; or a describing game, starting with 'I have a pretend cat, she is furry', he then has to add another adjective to describe the cat, and the list gets longer as you go back and forth.
- Get him thinking with questions such as 'What would happen if teddy came to life?' and talk about the possible outcomes, or on a more practical level 'Why do we shut the windows before we leave the house?'.
- Let him play with your kitchen scales, practising weighing and grouping items in order of weight.
- Give him problems to solve such as a treasure hunt following clues around the house, or a scavenger hunt to bring you a green item from each room in the house.

Should I worry? Is my child developing correctly?

See your doctor when your child is 5 years old if:

- he is falling over very regularly, perhaps more than his peers
- he does not make marks on paper in an attempt to draw
- he has unclear speech and is not understood by strangers or by his teacher
- he is not using tenses in his speech
- he does not interact with his peers or seems particularly withdrawn
- he cannot engage in imaginary play
- he has difficulty with eye contact
- he shows very extreme emotions frequently (such as extreme fear or agitation) or he does not show a range of emotions appropriately
- he does not attempt to dress or undress himself
- he is not toilet trained during the day
- he has an extremely short attention span (less than 5 minutes) or his teacher has concerns about his ability to engage in class
- he does not recognise his name printed on a page.

You should also see your doctor if he loses a skill that he has previously mastered.

The First Five Years covers, as the title suggests, the first 5 years of life and the huge changes in development for your child. Of course this does not mean that at 5 years old he is fully developed! There will be continuing physical changes as your child progresses from a child towards puberty, fine motor changes as he further develops hand control (to use, for example, for handwriting), language changes as his grammar and speech content develops, and social changes as he further discovers who he is and how he fits into the world.

Part 2

11

Sample activities

In this chapter you will find some suggestions for age- and stage-related play: these are simply suggestions and not blueprints for playing with your child. You will know best how to make your child laugh and have fun, and ultimately that is what playing is about! Although your child learns through play, having fun and bonding with your child is hugely important, making the learning almost a by-product of the playing itself. It is unlikely that you will wish to do these activities every time you sit down to play with your child, or go out with your child, and some of the suggested activities will turn simple household chores or other tasks into a longer activity. However, spending time on some of the suggested activities occasionally may help develop, for example, handling skills or sorting skills. Sometimes we all have to dash quickly into the shops and allowing your child to do a treasure hunt for a green vegetable may not be appropriate, but when you do have the time, this kind of play can make daily chores more fun for both you and your child.

For each scenario, approximate ages are given for when a child may be able to start playing in a particular way, for example being able to mix ingredients in a cooking bowl. These are suggestions; your child may be ready earlier or later than the ages given. As a child gets older, he does not have to stop doing an earlier activity if he still enjoys it. For example, if your child starts putting laundry in the washing machine at 2 years old, he does not have to stop doing this in order to match up socks at 3 years old: he can do both tasks if he is having fun!

None of the activities involves expensive equipment; you can simply use what you have around the house or in the garden or park. Not only are the games themselves fun and promote a particular skill but the talking around them develops your child's language and thinking skills. Try asking questions such as 'What are you doing?', 'Why are you doing that?', 'What do you think will happen next?' and 'What else could you do here?'. Also model the language for particular games; for example if you are hunting for toys in a tub of pasta, you are 'putting your hands *in* the pasta', '*digging* to the bottom' or 'pulling toys *out* of the tub'.

Finally, use your imagination and let your child use his: the possibilities for games and adventures are as limitless as your imagination, so have fun!

Keeping moving

Your child should be as active as possible and avoid long periods of physical inactivity. Once your child can walk on his own the current recommendation is that he is active for at least 3 hours every day. (For children over 5 years old, this is reduced to a minimum of an hour a day.) Although 3 hours may seem like a long time, it does not mean constant high-octane physical activity. Low-level physical activities such as pottering about playing at home or in the garden all count and can be spread over the course of the day! The amount of time that your child spends sitting down should be limited. This includes the amount of time sitting in a buggy, car seat and on the sofa in front of the television. This does not mean that he should not spend time sitting down doing activities or reading books – rather, this is actively encouraged – but it needs to be balanced against other activities that are more active.

Before your child is able to walk alone, there are no guidelines regarding the time he should spend being active. Nevertheless it is important to give plenty of opportunity and space for tummy time, kicking, rolling, crawling and pulling himself up to an upright position. Rocking your young baby helps to develop his vestibular system which is involved in balance and is required to help him to stand and sit up when he is older. Try tummy time little and often; carry him in different positions to encourage head and neck control; and place him on a mat with a mobile or hold toys above him to encourage him to reach for them. As he gets older and begins to sit up and crawl, give him plenty of opportunities, encouragement and praise for physical efforts.

Suggested activities for when your child can walk alone include the following.

- Play at home: as he crawls after toy trains and cars, stands up to get a toy, squats down to put it on the floor, picks it up again, he is generally continually active and does not sit still for long! You can encourage this further by having races such as picking up toy bricks from one side of the room and placing them in their container on the other side of the room. Dancing to music, jumping on a trampoline and playing in the garden are great forms of physical activity. Other games to play at home to keep him active include: Follow the Leader and Simon Says; trying to imitate walking like animals; and songs with actions such as 'Heads, shoulders, knees and toes' or 'Row, row, row your boat'.
- Get him out of the buggy as much as you can: but of course there will be times when this is not appropriate. For example, when he is 2 years old, he may need the buggy for a 20 minute walk to a sibling's school because he is not fast enough to get there on time; but once the older child is in school, he can then do the walk home. You may need the buggy for a long walk to the shops, but once you are there let him out to walk beside you. This often means that the walk takes longer, as you will move at his pace and probably spend time looking at ants, leaves and anything else that takes his fancy. Conversely, it might mean that you end up running!
- Visit your local park: this does not always have to mean the playground. Other ideas include: taking nature walks; going on trips to kick autumn leaves, or to collect pine cones or conkers; blowing bubbles for him to chase; doing bark rubbings; and taking a magnifying glass and a small pot to see if you can catch (and release) any mini beasts. When you are in the playground, let him run around, making full use of the equipment, which will involve climbing, balancing and swinging. Bring along a ball for ball play; throwing, catching and kicking.
- Use scooters, balance bikes or conventional bikes: these also teach a new skill as well as being great forms of exercise.

- Swim: he will love being in the water!
- Go to your local indoor soft play centre: also check whether your local Sure Start centre offers any physical activity classes.
- Encourage the whole family to be more active: go for a walk at the weekend or play ball games together.

Imaginative/role play

Imaginative play or role play is essentially when your child pretends that he or an object is something or someone else. For example, when he pretends to be a doctor or he imagines that a toy building brick is a computer. Role play is another example of learning through play; not only is he learning to handle the objects he is playing with, but also his speech and language are developing as he talks during the games and so he develops his social skills. Role play encourages your child to see things from another person or object's point of view. It helps with his general understanding of the world around him and can also help him to deal with potentially fearful situations as it gives him a sense of control. For example, when he pretends to be a doctor he is showing that he understands what a doctor does, as well as perhaps working through his emotions about having a vaccination.

Ideas for role play include the following.

- Hold a tea party: from approximately 1 year old, you, your child and perhaps some teddies can have a tea party, using either a toy tea set or some plastic cups that you already have. The props themselves are not as important as the play itself – you can pretend that anything is a cup of tea and a piece of cake!
- Pretend to be an animal: swing your arm like an elephant's trunk, buzz like a bee and flap your arms to fly like a bird. There are lots of songs that can also encourage role play: for example, you can pretend to be each animal in 'Old Macdonald had a farm' or you can put a doll to bed in 'Miss Polly had a dolly who was sick'.
- Role play daily activities: at about 1 to 2 years old and onwards, you can role play such daily activities as cleaning teddy's teeth or brushing dolly's hair, as well as feeding them and changing their nappies.

- Encourage social skills in more complex imaginative play: as he gets older, role play can involve skills such as dressing and undressing with soft toys and acting out different scenarios that he has experienced himself or seen in books (mummy, doctor, dentist, fireman, pilot, zoo keeper, etc.). He will probably have to be the central role (playing the daddy) and you, or a soft toy or other object, will have the secondary role (playing the baby).
- Use simple household objects as props: set up pillows and blankets for teddies who are ill in bed and use an old medicine syringe or spoon to give them medicine. You could use plastic plates and cutlery to set up an imaginary restaurant; or use old unopened junk mail, unused return envelops or old stamps to play post office; and use a can of shaving foam and a lollipop stick to be a barber.
- Employ one object to represent another: imaginative play does not have to be just about playing people or animals, but also about using objects. Pretend that his cup is a camera and take a picture.
- Model behaviour in various social situations: role play can also be useful to encourage turn taking.

Arts and crafts

You do not have to be 'arty' to get down (and dirty!) with your child, enjoying arts and crafts. Nor does your child have to produce perfect masterpieces. It is not the outcome that matters, but rather it is the process itself which is important, along with the skills and creativity that he uses to create his artwork. So if he tells you that the black splodge on the page is a monster, then to him it is and you can praise him for it. If he asks you what colour the grass should be, you do not necessarily have to say green, you could ask him what colour he wants it to be (after all, the grass could be pink in his imagination). Do not worry if he cannot colour within the lines; this skill requires a lot of hand control and will come later with practice. The skills required for arts and crafts include: core strength to sit or stand for a period of time to create the artwork; handling skills to draw, paint, cut or glue; and imagination and creativity. Language skills will develop as you talk about what he is doing and why.

Some parents and carers are concerned about the mess involved in painting and other craft activities. If so, try covering the table in newspaper, lay a cheap shower curtain or plastic tablecloth on the floor to catch any bits (because they are easily wiped clean) and pop on an apron to protect clothes.

The following is a list of different arts and crafts activities, along with examples at each age, although the possibilities are endless!

- Draw and paint: this can be started as soon as he can hold a pen in his fist and make a mark on a page! Initially you may find that it is easier for him to use a crayon or a felt-tip marker as these will make a bright, strong effect on the page without needing as much pressure applied to them as a pencil. With time you will notice that his grip on the pen or crayon changes from holding it in his fist to holding it between his fingers and that his scribbles change from linear scribbles to circular scribbles, and then he will be able to draw circles before progressing to other shapes. Painting is another great method of encouraging mark making – use big brushes and bright colours. As his skills develop he may be able to start to use other painting tools such as stampers, rollers, sponges, vegetable prints and bits of string or a cotton bud. When he is older, he may enjoy pottery or glass painting. He will enjoy art on a large scale: try covering your kitchen table with paper and then paint on the plates, cutlery and some food!
- Use playdough: from approximately 1 year old he will be able to start to play with playdough, and you can even make your own (see the Appendix). Initially this will be a tactile sensory experience as he squishes the playdough in his hands and between his fingers. He will enjoy the different colours, though he will not be able to keep the colours separate for quite a while yet! As his handling skills improve he will start to be able to: pinch small pieces of dough from a larger portion; squash the dough flat with his hands and then roll it out using a rolling pin; and use cutters to create shapes. After being shown, he will then be able to separate off small portions and roll them into balls or sausage shapes. There are various 'tools' available such as shape cutters, stampers, rolling pins and rolling cutters, syringes which create different shapes and many more, all of which develop handling skills. As his skills improve further he can cut the playdough with a plastic knife or plastic scissors, and pick up small pieces with child's tweezers. The play will become more imaginative and creative, for example making play food for a picnic

or creating animals. Other examples of a modelling clay product include Play-Doh™ or Plasticine™ (which is firmer), or you could use pastry dough, bread dough, saltdough (which can be formed into shapes, left to dry or baked, and then painted and decorated – see the Appendix for a recipe) and clay.

- Cut, glue and stick: make collages using glue and pieces of paper, foam shapes, dried foodstuffs such as pasta, rice or beans, glitter, old sequins, buttons or beads, pipe cleaners, leaves, pine cones or anything else you can find! Initially he will concentrate on the skills required to pick up an item, apply the glue and stick it on the collage, but he will become more focused on what it is he is creating as his skills improve. Stickers are also great for handling skills: he might not be able to peel the sticker off its sheet, but he can stick it on some paper if you hand one to him. Other ideas for projects include making masks with paper plates or crowns with card, as well as posters to put on the wall or the fridge. Encourage cutting skills using child-safe scissors: at first he will cut whatever shapes he wants, but by 4 years old he can cut around circular shapes and by 5 years old he can cut around more linear shapes with corners. Try cutting pictures out of magazines, catalogues or birthday cards to make a collage.
- Sew and string beads: between 2 to 3 years old he will start to be able to string large beads on a string or a lace and will start to be able to use a lace to sew, for example on sewing cards. Alternatives to using beads include stringing pasta or circular cereal such as Cheerios™ onto string, or even liquorice strings, for a treat, or threading fruit on to bamboo skewers to make fruit kebabs. As his handling skills develop he will be able to use smaller beads with smaller holes and will become more dextrous at sewing. Threading beads onto a string is a good opportunity to talk about colours and numbers: for example, you could ask a 3-year-old to put on a red bead first, then to select a blue bead, etc., while a 4-year-old could make a simple pattern, putting on three red beads, then two blue, etc.

At the supermarket

A trip to the supermarket is not just an opportunity to pick up some food and other household items for the week. To your child it is a treasure trove of goodies and an opportunity for some great developmental play along the way. During the entire trip you will be teaching him social skills by displaying the behaviour expected in a supermarket: no shouting, no knocking over displays, no eating produce or stealing – but how to be polite to the cashier, how to pay and how to walk safely to the car, using safety and observational skills. The list is endless and it is just a simple trip to the shops!

Even though your baby, within the first few months of life, may look like he is simply lying on the baby support, he will actually be stimulated by all the lights, colours and sounds around him. No matter how old your baby is, keep talking to him and describe what you are doing. As your child grows, he can be involved in your shopping trip in the following ways.

- 9 months old: he has learnt to sit up, so sitting in the child seat of a supermarket trolley lets him practise this gross motor skill. As his handling skills develop further he will be able to hold produce and learn about different textures and shapes.
- 18 months old: start counting with him. For example, count out how many oranges you need, or let him put them in a bag, counting along with you.
- 2 years old: give him a small notepad and pencil and let him practise his fine motor or handling skills by scribbling his own shopping list.
- Between the ages of 2 and 3 years: instigate a treasure hunt to find objects of different colours or shapes. Questions such as 'Can you find a green vegetable?' develop his observational and sorting skills. You could let him help to push the trolley as you point out items for him to take off the shelves and put in, which is a good physical activity.
- 3 years old: make a shopping list of pictures for him to match with the produce. This will introduce him to the idea that marks on a page have meaning.
- 4 years old: he may be able to recognise numbers, so try writing a numbered shopping list and letting him cross off items as you buy.
- 5 years old: take him on a digital photo treasure hunt, asking him to take pictures of the objects you need. This will develop his fine motor skills in handling the camera, as well as observational skills and puzzle-solving skills.

Outdoor activities

Your child will love to be outside no matter the weather, so wrap up warm and pop on a hood if it is cold and wet – but still head outdoors! The outside environment provides a multitude of opportunities for exploration and discovery as well as the chance to experience a different environment, fresh air and light, and some physical activity. If you do not have a garden there are multiple community open spaces outside; your local park is a fantastic resource, not just for its playground.

Here are some suggestions for outdoor activities to try as your child grows.

- From birth: he loves to be outside. If it is warm, lay him on a blanket on the ground, or wrap him up snug if it is colder. Put him under a tree to watch the pattern of the light and the leaves or branches as they gently move in the breeze. Let him listen to the sound of the leaves rustling, the birds singing or even the cars moving down the street. This is all stimulation as he begins his discovery of the world.
- Crawling babies: ignore the dirt and let him roam. The outside world provides a range of textures to feel, from hard paving stones to soft grass, and the rough feel of tree bark.
- 1 year old: MUD! He loves exploring in the earth and mud; other good materials for outside play are sand and water. Initially he will simply feel them in his hands and between his fingers. Bubbles are also a great sensory experience, starting from looking at them, to popping them using one finger, to blowing them himself.
- 2 years old: he can dig in the sand or dirt, perhaps using a rake to encourage both strength and handling skills. Hide small objects in the sand or dirt for him to discover. When he is older, encourage him to bury objects for you to find, which encourages problem-solving and cognitive skills.
- Between the ages of 2 and 3 years: encourage outside physical activity. Let him walk on low walls (keep hold of one hand!) or jump between paving stones. As he gets older he could try walking in a straight line on the paving stones, perhaps following a crack between the stones.
- From 2 to 3 years old: introduce gardening. Using an old yoghurt pot and a plastic spoon, ask him to fill it with earth, use a finger

to poke a hole in which to plant a seed, cover the seed with soil, water it and watch it grow. You can even grow cress (very quickly) on some cotton wool! Gardening encourages multiple areas of development: for example, the handling skills required to use a spoon or small trowel to fill the pot with earth, and the dexterity required to poke a hole for the seed. It also requires patience and nurturing: he needs to remember to give the seed water – but not to drown it!

- 3 years old: set up an outside obstacle course for him, using a hoop or a piece of string to lay out a course. Try to include obstacles to jump over, climb over, roll over and crawl over or through. Run races (forwards, backwards and crawling) and see how many jumps he can do in 10 seconds. Build a den for him, using a tent, sheet or even a cardboard box, to provide multiple opportunities for imaginative play. Let him paint the box for his den and decorate it as he wants. Perhaps he will hold a tea party for the worms he has found or the birds he can see: maybe he will let you into his hideout, but maybe not!

- 4 years old: the simple gardening such as that described above can also lead to some easy science experiments, such as 'What does a seed need to grow?'. Try using a selection of yoghurt pots and seeds: put one in the light and another in the dark, give one water and leave one to dry, and give one soil and one nothing. Experiments such as these are great for developing problem-solving skills.

The following activities are suitable at any age.

- Outdoor art: this could include collecting materials from outside (such as earth, sand, grasses or leaves) to make a collage, or bark rubbing: take a piece of paper, hold it against various trees and rub with a crayon to make different patterns for a picture. Drawing chalk pictures on paving stones or a fence (chalks will wash out in the rain) strengthens his core and legs as he squats to chalk on the floor, and improves his handling skills as he scribbles with the chalk. Encourage him to use big hand and arm movements to make marks in the earth, mud or sand as a precursor to writing: he could even use a stick to make the marks. Try 'painting' the fence or the outside of your house with water, using a big brush or roller, which again encourages the arm strength required for writing and is also great fun that can be done over and over again as the water dries. A fence is a great prop as the wood darkens with the water 'paint' and then returns to the previous colour as it dries.

- Bug hunting: he may find the world of insects and mini beasts fascinating. During outside explorations he is likely to find worms, woodlice and other insects. He is more likely to be curious than frightened, so even if you find insects difficult, try not to communicate this. Let him see you handle a worm, ladybird or snail, being gentle not to hurt them and always putting them back where you found them. Talk about what you have found: the snail's hard shell and the worm's long wriggling body. Let him discover the outside world with all its inhabitants! He may have lots of questions about insects, plants or other aspects of being outside; you can help answer these and support his discoveries by reading books about insects, plants and other creatures. Tape two empty toilet rolls together to create your own binoculars to add to the experience!

Household chores

Your child is extremely keen to be helpful and the household chores will always need to be done, so playing with him while doing the chores can make them both more interesting for you and stimulating for him! The list below describes activities that can be done during household tasks to make them fun and interesting, while also allowing you to get on with the job at hand. There are also tasks which your child will begin to be able to do himself, initially with supervision and then increasingly independently. You are not putting your child to work as such, rather teaching him responsibility for his toys and other objects in the house. By encouraging him to partake in some simple chores you also teach him that the family work together as a team, all with different roles to play within that team: your child will feel needed and that he is contributing to the family. The skills of doing the tasks themselves will encourage mobility, handling skills and problem-solving skills. Give lots of praise and do not set the standard too high: he may drop a plate he is carrying to the sink and create more mess, but he was trying to help! It is never too early to start, so encourage your child to help put away toys from an early age as part of the game of playing.

- 1 year old: even laundry can be a sensory experience, sitting in the washing basket feeling all the different textures of the clothes around him. If you are washing up, pop him in an apron and give him a small washing-up bowl with water and some small cups to use for pouring.
- From 18 months to 2 years old: let him have a go at dusting when you are doing the cleaning: he may be moving the dust around but he feels involved. Instead of using a duster, pop a pair of old socks on his hands for him to dust with. He loves copying you in role play: he may like to play with smaller toy versions of the equipment you use for cleaning (mops, dusters or vacuum cleaners).
- 2 years old: at laundry time he will be able to help you lift clothes out of the laundry basket and into the machine. With direction, he will be able to sort them out into dark and light colour loads. He can pull wet laundry out of the machine, into the basket and then into the dryer, which is great for improving strength.
- From 2 to 3 years old: he will be able to pull up the covers on his cot/ bed, pick up and put away his toys and help unload the dishwasher (especially items like Tupperware™, plastic plates or cutlery). As always, be sure to give lots of praise when he does a job. You can make these activities into games: taking it in turns to put blocks away or racing to see who can put their pile of blocks away first. If you have pets he will be able to start to help put out food for them, and brush them if required.
- From 3 to 4 years old: laundry time can be used as a tool for sorting games, matching up socks or whose clothes go in which pile. If you have clothes pegs, let him practise putting them on the washing line, which is great for hand strength and dexterity. He may also be able to fold simple items of clothing such as underwear or tea towels and be able to put them away. He can carry out other simple chores such as laying paper napkins on the table, or even learning to set the table. He can carry his empty plate to the dishwasher or sink, and will start to be able to wash up: for example, washing paint pots with supervision (which can take as long, and be as much fun, as the painting activity itself!). He will be able to help carry in and put away shopping – though obviously start with rolls of toilet paper and not cartons of eggs!

Cooking activities

Cooking is a fantastic activity to do with your little one; not only will it encourage multiple skills such as core strength, handling and problem solving, but it is also an opportunity for bonding, having fun and teaching him about food – where it comes from and how it appears on the table ready to eat! Since you are making food for him anyway, involving him in the process makes it easier to get on with the task (without him pulling you away to play with something else). He is also more likely to eat the final product if he has been engaged with, and enjoyed the process of, making the food. As always, remember to consider safety: he needs supervision with knives and other sharp kitchen objects and you will need to talk him about the oven being hot.

Cooking can start from planning the meal or recipe, making a list of ingredients (a shopping list of pictures for a 3-year-old to cross off), going to the shops, finding the ingredients on the shelves, putting them in the basket, paying for them, taking them out of the bags at home, getting everything ready (including yourselves by washing hands) – all before the actual cooking process itself! Cooking encourages handling skills and coordination: mixing, whisking, rolling, pouring, stirring, cutting, grating and peeling. Also needed are numeracy skills: counting, measuring, weighing; and vocabulary skills as you talk about the process, science, geography, cultural identity and even history of the dish! When the cooking is done, clearing up, setting the table and eating together encourages social development.

Talk about the ingredients, where they come from and what they look like before they arrive in the packet: for example the journey from wheat to flour, or even that a potato grows underground, while an apple grows on a tree. You can then talk about the changes that happen during the cooking process: after all, the process that turns cake batter to cake looks like magic! It is an opportunity to start to discuss healthy eating and healthy living, that you eat fruit and vegetables daily but not cake. You can also use cooking as a way to practise sharing and taking turns (you have a turn mixing and then he does).

Here are some ways of involving your growing child in cooking and encouraging him to enjoy his food.

- From 6 to 18 months old: eating is a sensory experience. No matter what your age, the enjoyment of the final product is as much about its smell, appearance and feel in your mouth as it is about the taste itself. The same is true of the cooking process, in which smell and touch is important. Bowls of rice, beans and pasta are great for tactile stimulation and if you want to get messier, try flour or water. Let him smell the herbs or spices before you add them to the pot. And when he is bored of the food, let him explore the pots and pans: there is lots of fun to be had with a set of pans, measuring cups or bowls and a wooden spoon! This is not just making noise but also exploring and learning ('If I bang this here it makes one noise, but if I bang it there it sounds different'), as well as developing handling skills.
- 18 months old: mixing ingredients together with a spoon makes him a part of the process. Hold the bowl steady if you do not want ingredients everywhere!
- 2 years old: let him get really stuck in. He can pull a piece of dough off a larger section, and roll it to create a ball or sausage shape, mash potatoes with a masher, and turn on the mixer (with supervision). Let him hold the bag of sugar to see how heavy it is, and pour ingredients into a bowl. Count out ingredients as you go: the number of eggs or spoonfuls of flour needed.
- 3 years old: introduce more maths skills. Count out ingredients and use scales to weigh them, to help with number recognition. Explore the concept of weight by comparing which ingredient is heavier: for example, by holding a bag of flour and a bag of sugar. Handling skills include: pouring ingredients from a jug or spoon into a bowl, mixing ingredients, using a rolling pin to roll out dough or bash biscuits to crumbs, and using a plastic knife to cut soft cheese or butter a slice of bread. Play games such as guessing the ingredient from the smell or the taste.
- 4 years old: initially with supervision, he may be able to use a vegetable peeler to peel carrots or a knife to chop cheese or fruit (starting with a soft fruit such as a piece of melon). Encourage him to eat fruit by letting him chop some fruit into bite-size pieces and then thread them onto a bamboo skewer to produce fruit kebabs. If you want to encourage further maths skills, get him to create a pattern: grape, melon, grape, melon and so on. Handling skills at this age also include cracking eggs into a bowl or using a melon baller.

Pasta play

Pasta is a source of hours of fun! For some of the examples below you could also use rice, flour or beans. Pasta is cheap and can be stored and reused time and time again. To dye uncooked pasta, use a small amount of food colouring and some vinegar to set the dye; spread out the pasta and leave it to dry completely.

- 1 year old: cook some spaghetti and run it under cold water to cool it down quickly. Add a small amount of oil to keep it slippery and plop the whole lot onto a tray for some slimy, gooey sensory play. He will love the feel of the sticky strands running through his fingers. You could divide the spaghetti into plastic bags and add some food colouring to make rainbow pasta. If some spaghetti goes into his mouth, it does not matter!
- Between the ages of 1 and 2 years: have a pasta sensory tub using uncooked pasta of differing shapes and sizes, perhaps dyed different colours, and hide small objects (such as cars or plastic animals) inside it. He will love plunging his hands into the tub and all the sensations he feels as he does so before pulling out a surprise! You could then use the small car or digger to pick up pieces of pasta. In order to encourage problem-solving skills as well as handling skills, also give him a spoon, an old toilet roll tube and some small cups and containers. Let him explore: mixing, stirring, pouring from one cup into another and popping the pasta into the tube and watching it fall out of the other end. Also get him to listen to the sound as he pours the pasta from one tub into another. The possibilities for exploration are endless!
- 2 years old: start to use pasta and other store cupboard ingredients for collage making. Use some PVA glue and get sticking! You could also paint cooked spaghetti, or other uncooked pasta shapes, to create colourful pasta art.
- Between the ages of 2 and 3 years: using a bag of tricolour pasta of the same shape, or white pasta of a few different shapes, he can try to sort the pasta by colour or shape. He can sort the pasta into little bowls or an empty egg carton. As he gets older you can make it more complicated by combining pasta of different colours *and* different shapes in order to develop problem-solving skills.
- 3 years old: try a kitchen science experiment. For example, cook some spaghetti but do not add any oil to keep it soft: instead, add a little

water. Over time he will notice that the pasta begins to dry out and needs a little more water to keep it malleable. Handling skills can be improved when he cuts the pasta with child-safe scissors or a plastic knife, twists it onto a fork, or picks it up with a pair of kitchen tongs. Add in some imaginative play: 'What are you playing with?' (worms, snakes or vines for example), 'Why are the snakes here?' and 'Why are you chopping them?'. Another activity is to make bracelets or necklaces by stringing pasta tubes or other shapes onto a piece of string (you could also use round cereal such as Cheerios™).

- 4 years old: continue to play the pasta-sorting games, but use a pair of large tweezers or child chopsticks. This encourages hand dexterity and strength, which is essential for writing.

Puzzle play

Puzzles are a fantastic source of learning opportunities for your child. They help with many skills: problem solving; handling and coordination (as he turns the shapes all around to get them to fit); memory (the puzzle gets easier the more times he does it); cognition (such as shape, colour, number and letter recognition, depending on what the puzzle is); and even social skills (turn taking and working collaboratively to complete the puzzle). The problem-solving skills required also help him to begin to deal with the concept of making mistakes, or failing, but then continuing to try until he succeeds in completing the puzzle. The ability to try, and keep trying despite mistakes, is essential for his later learning. At the beginning you have to give lots of help, but your child will become increasingly independent with puzzles – though keep up the praise and encouragement!

Here are some suggestions for playing with puzzles as your child grows.

- From 6 to 9 months old and onwards: he will be able to start putting objects into containers and pulling them out again. Shape-sorter toys then further develop this skill (when he puts shapes through the matching shaped hole). This is a great way to introduce the concept of shapes and colours, as well as the skills required to match the correct piece to the correct hole, and the handling skills needed to turn the piece and fit it into the hole.

- 18 months old: try peg puzzles. These are often made of wood, where wooden shapes with pegs to use as handles need to be inserted into slots cut out of a wooden board.
- 2 years old: he is ready to try very simple two- to four-piece jigsaw puzzles. Over time, the number of pieces and complexity of the puzzle will increase: by 3 years old he will be able to complete four- to eight-piece puzzles on his own and more difficult ones with help.

Listening games

Your child may often hear what you are saying, but he is not truly listening. The following games can help increase listening skills and the ability to concentrate and pay attention. At the start of each game, you may want to remind your child that he needs to listen carefully.

- Guess the sound: pop a blindfold on him or ask him to cover his eyes, then create a simple household noise, such as running the vacuum cleaner, and ask him to identify the sound. Other sounds you could make include running a tap, boiling a kettle, the telephone ringing, tapping on a keyboard and shutting a door. You can also play this by using your voice to recreate sounds (in which case he does not need to cover his eyes); for example, guess the animal noise – take turns to play!
- Nursery rhyme mistakes: recite a nursery rhyme but change a word and he has to point out your mistake. For example, 'Little Bo Peep lost her horse'.
- Simon Says: issue a command to do something, such as 'Simon says touch your head', and he has to follow the instruction unless you omit the 'Simon says'. This is a great game for not only following instructions but also remembering that unless you say 'Simon says' he does not have to do it! Make your commands as silly as possible!
- Action missions: give him instructions to complete a mission. For example, 'Hop three times and then sit on the floor', or 'Bring me your toothbrush'. As he gets older, the missions can become more complicated. Be sure to reward a completed mission!
- Chinese Whispers or the telephone game: whisper a sentence or a few words near his ear and ask him to repeat what you said. To make

it more difficult, ask him to whisper it on to someone else before they repeat it.

- Traffic Lights: this is a variation of Musical Bumps or Musical Statues without the music. Ask him to perform an action, such as swinging his arms, clapping or jumping; but he can only start when you say 'Green light!' and he must stop immediately when you say 'Red light!'.
- Clapping games: clap out a rhythm (start with a simple one) and then he has to clap the rhythm back. Take turns to start.
- Follow the Leader: this is not an auditory listening game but a visual one. He still has to concentrate and follow the instructions.

12

Common concerns

As much as we all like to think that our child is a perfect specimen, he can also be extremely challenging! This chapter aims to cover some common parental concerns and behavioural issues regarding a child under 5 years old. If appropriate, a developmental explanation will be given as to why the behaviour is happening: but sometimes just the knowledge that your child is not being malicious, or out to get you, but is simply being an average X-year-old can help you to deal with a situation in a calm manner. It is extremely difficult to deal with the emotions that can affect your judgement when dealing with your child and this chapter is not meant to be dictatorial regarding parenting. You may well have another method of dealing with inappropriate behaviour; after all, you know your child best! Yet your emotions when dealing with your child can make it easy to fall into habits and you may find it difficult to cope with bad behaviour or other arduous issues: for this reason, tips and advice on how to deal with the behaviour are given. As always, if you are concerned that your child's behaviour is more extreme, seek advice from your doctor. Also remember that practice makes perfect, so you will need to repeat each behaviour management technique over and over again to reinforce the message.

Separation anxiety

Separation anxiety is a normal part of childhood development and tends to peak at approximately 9 to 18 months of age, though it can start a few months earlier. It tends to lessen by about 2 years old. Your very young baby is extremely sociable and under approximately 6 months old will happily beam at strangers and go to them to be held without protest. However, by about 9 months old you may notice that your child becomes increasingly nervous or clingy around strangers (or even anyone that is not you!). He may become distressed when you leave; to go to work, to leave his bedroom at night, and sometimes even if you leave a room momentarily. He now knows how important you are and how much he needs you, and he has also become aware that you are separate from him. It is therefore only natural that he will become distressed when you leave him because he does not know that you will come back again. Even as he gets older and begins to understand better that you will come back, he does not yet have a concept of time so will not understand when that will be: a minute or an hour can both seem endless! Although a normal part of development, separation anxiety can be upsetting and frustrating for all involved, both for you as a parent and for your baby.

Be sure to give your baby lots of attention, hugs and reassurance when you are there, and even from a very early age you can start practising the concept that Mummy goes away but comes back again. A great way of doing this is with Peek-a-boo games, or you can let him crawl on his own to another room for a few minutes. You can also practise by warning him that you are going to leave but will be back in a few minutes, for example when you are going to the toilet. If your child is attending a new nursery or has a new carer, then give them time to get to know one another when you are there to give reassurance. Perhaps have a few sessions where you stay at the nursery for an hour or so before leaving for increasing lengths of time. These trial sessions should be taken at a time when your child is not hungry, tired or unwell because these will only make it tougher!

The moment of acute distress for your child is often the moment that you leave, so when it is time to leave, give him a kiss and a cuddle, say your goodbye and tell him that you will be back later. Making a good routine or ritual can also be helpful, such as a particular goodbye phrase or wave. Even if you hear your child crying it is not helpful for you to return and have repeated or protracted goodbyes, which will prolong his distress and add to his confusion because he does not understand when exactly you are leaving or coming back – but he does quickly understand that if he cries you will return for an extra hug. Your child will be able to pick up on your own distress so, as hard as it can be, try not to show him that you are also finding the process hard. Many are the times that a parent runs out of the door to the sound of a crying baby and needs a little cry too! Hard as it may be, being consistent and calm will help. For your child, the distress at separation is short lived and the tears often stop within a few minutes (though sometimes start again when he sees you at the end of the day). If you are worried about your child, telephone the carer a little later in the day so you can be reassured that he is alright. Although this upset may last only a few minutes it is important that you do say goodbye and go through the process of leaving so that your child is aware that you have gone. If you slip out unnoticed, when he is engaged with a toy, he will not understand that you have gone and this can cause more distress later in the day. If your child has a comforter such as a special teddy, let him have it to comfort him.

If your child's separation anxiety is extreme, for example with physical symptoms such as vomiting or diarrhoea, or it disrupts his sleep, seek further advice from your doctor. However, separation anxiety usually eases when your child is older, more independent and understands that you will always come back.

Clinging

Clinginess is not necessarily the same as separation anxiety (as already described). Certainly your child may cling at times of separation but he may also be clingy when you are staying. Your child becomes clingy when he is anxious, for example about a new situation or person, an animal or a loud noise. It can seem like a sudden change from when your baby would crawl or toddle away from you, seemingly oblivious to any lurking dangers, to a toddler who is literally attached to you at the hip. This is because he has realised that the world is a huge and unknown place! Your toddler is torn – he wants to become more independent but the world is scary: something that looks soft may be hard and hurt him, an insect may sting, an animal may scratch, or he may tumble over and bang his arm. As he ventures further away from you to become more independent, he also needs more reassurance. Although clinging can be frustrating, it shows that you make your child feel safe and secure. You may notice that your child swings from wanting to do everything himself without help to being very clingy, as he bounces between independence and being dependent on you.

Depending on his age and language skills your child may or may not be able to express his anxieties, so try to help him. For example, if you notice that he becomes clingy when a dog passes him in the street, ask him if he is worried about the dog. If he says yes, help him to put into words what specifically worries him (is it the dog's teeth or the way in which the dog jumps up?). Then give lots of reassurance that you are there to keep him safe and that the dog is friendly.

Make sure that you also give lots of attention to positive emotions so that he understands that he does not only receive attention if he is feeling anxious. Do not force him to do anything that scares him because this may lead to failure and negative feelings, worsening the situation. There is an instinct to say that there is nothing to be afraid of, be it of an animal, a monster under the bed or nightmare, but to your child that is simply not true – he is afraid. Instead give him the comfort and reassurance that he needs and a tool to help him to deal with the fear. For example, if he is scared of monsters under the bed give him an imaginary (or real) magic wand with which to protect himself. Telling stories and reading books can also help him to deal with anxiety. Remember that your child copies you, so try to stay calm and reassuring during new activities, and even in situations that may make you anxious, such as dealing with spiders!

If you are unable to calm and reassure your child, or if his anxiety appears so extreme that he cannot function (disrupting sleep or making him unable to play), then speak to your doctor.

Attention seeking

Attention seeking can take many forms: from clinging (as already described), to whining, complaining, being aggressive, kicking, biting, behaving inappropriately to show off, or a continual request to 'watch me', 'look at me', 'help me' and 'play with me'. Your child will most likely show attention-seeking behaviour of one sort or another at some point. As to why, he simply wants more attention, admittedly sometimes more that you can give at a particular moment in time. If he cannot achieve his desires (i.e. your focus and attention) with good behaviour, he will use bad behaviour because any attention is better than nothing at all, even if it is negative attention, focused on shouting, time outs or punishments. This is not to say that you have to lavish 100% attention and focus on your child at all times: he has to learn that you also have needs and that you are not able to focus on him constantly, or that you are doing something for the good of everyone, for example preparing a meal. There are no guidelines as to how much attention your child needs. Rather, that his needs are balanced against your ability and time available to give to him.

First, be sure that there is no physical reason for the behaviour. For example, if your child whinges and whines when he has to put on his shoes, complaining that he doesn't want to walk, then check that his shoes are a good fit because he may not be able to pinpoint this problem for himself. Try to observe if the attention-seeking behaviour occurs at specific trigger points, for example when the telephone rings or if you pay attention to a sibling or other child. If it does, then you can talk about this, encouraging him to wait and reassuring him that you will spend time with him afterwards. Be specific with your young child who has no concept of time: for example, 'Let me help your brother with this puzzle and then we can do one together'.

Make sure that your child does have quality uninterrupted time with you, without telephone calls, text messages and emails. Tell him how much you enjoy being with him, what fun you are having, and reassure and repeat how much you love him. This does not have to be for hours: 5 minutes of focused one-to-one time (reading a story, having a cuddle or playing a game together) will help him to feel that you do pay him attention. Tell him how much you are looking forward to your special time with him, how much you enjoyed it and how you cannot wait until you have your special time again tomorrow. Focus on the positives and not the negatives: notice and praise good behaviour little and often. If there is bad behaviour, do not focus on it with shouting or recriminations, but quietly and calmly use a time out and tell him that what he did was inappropriate. At the end of the time out remind him that you love him and then welcome him back into playing, remembering to lavish praise for good behaviour. If you do not feel that a time out is appropriate, then ignore the bad behaviour but point out that you are doing so: for example, 'I won't talk to you until you stop screeching'. If you find that you are too irritated to do this calmly, then have a time out yourself; leave the room and take some deep breaths so that you are calm enough to deal with the situation without escalating it further. As with all things, this takes practice, so be consistent and keep going!

Whining and whinging

Whining and whinging can be hugely frustrating and irritating for a parent, but essentially your child is trying to attract your attention and communicate something to you. Your child may have temper tantrums, may whine – or may do both! For a young child with a conflicting maelstrom of emotions that feel overwhelming, combined with the fact that he is easily frustrated, and he does not necessarily understand why he cannot have and do everything that he wants, the end result is often whining.

First, exclude common triggers for whinging such as thirst, hunger or tiredness. Then, as with all behaviours which you do not want to encourage, avoid paying it attention, be it positive or negative. It can be helpful to acknowledge that your child wants or needs something and then show him how you would like him to behave. For example, 'We don't whine, if you would like a drink then please say "Mummy I would like a drink please"'. By the time your child is 3 or 4 years old he can understand that his actions have consequences, so try: 'I can't understand/hear/won't listen to you because you are whining, if you speak normally/ask nicely I'll try to listen'.

As with all behaviour techniques, be consistent: giving in (and we have all done it) teaches your child that if he persists, he will get what he wants. Give plenty of positive attention to him and when he asks nicely without whining, remember to praise him for his good behaviour!

Tantrums

Tantrums – the meltdown where your child is lying on the supermarket floor, red in the face, kicking and screaming – are extremely common. They generally start after 1 year of age, culminating in the 'terrible twos' before generally subsiding after 3 years old. Your child may have 'anger tantrums', where he kicks, screams, bites and seems furious, or he may have 'distress tantrums', where he cries, screams, whines and seems inconsolably sad and upset. He may even display both kinds of behaviour during a tantrum. Tantrums occur when your child becomes aware of his needs, wants and desires but does not yet have enough language to explain them to you. He may want a drink or a nappy change but is not able to tell you; or he may not yet have the emotional maturity to understand what it is that he feels and needs. He may feel sad but not know what 'sadness' is and so a cuddle may help him to feel better. Tantrums can also be the result of frustration ('I want a chocolate') and he cannot understand why you would say no! Sometimes life is all just too much: the continual bombardment that your child experiences with new situations, environments and people, and the continual battling desires of increasing independence and the need for reassurance and dependence are just too overwhelming. Here, your child cannot deal with the rush of emotions that he is feeling and these come out in a temper tantrum.

Prevention is better than cure, so watch out for common triggers for temper tantrums. Your child is more likely to have a tantrum if he is hungry, thirsty or tired, so if possible try to avoid a shopping trip around nap time or straight after nursery and be sure to think about the possibility of hunger or thirst when you are out and about. If your child has tantrums when it is time to finish playing (for example, for dinner or to go out), then give plenty of warning signals of what is about to happen and what is expected of him. However, instead of telling him that it is dinner time in 5 minutes, sit with him as he plays and say to him that when he has finished the puzzle it will be dinner time. This is because he will not know the length of 5 minutes, and whether you give him 5 minutes or not, he still wants to finish!

If you are aware of particular triggers for your child's tantrums, such as wanting a toy or object in the supermarket, then distraction will often prevent a meltdown: try singing a song or acting silly. At home, try another activity or quickly change the environment, for example 'Let's have a running race outside'. Another way to prevent tantrums is to give choice where it is appropriate. For example, if you have a daily battle about getting dressed, instead of saying that it is time to get dressed, or asking if he wants to get dressed and him saying a flat 'no', start with a statement of fact followed by a choice: 'It's time to get dressed now; would you like to wear the blue socks or the red socks?'. If he replies 'No socks' then you can respond that he has to wear socks but that he can choose the red or the blue ones. Your young child has very little control over his life: he does not decide where he goes, who with or what he does and so giving him some control over simple and little choices can prevent tantrums.

Watching your child have a tantrum is difficult for you: it can make you feel frustrated, embarrassed, cross, sad, anxious and worried all at once! The instinct is sometimes to give in to stop the behaviour ('Yes, you can have the chocolate'), but whether it took you 1 minute or 5 minutes to agree to his demand, it has reinforced the idea for your child that having a tantrum results in him getting his own way, even though it takes a certain amount of screaming. So once you have made a decision, be consistent and stick to it. You can empathise with your child: 'I understand you're cross with me but it's lunch time and you can't have a chocolate', but you must ignore the bad behaviour, difficult as this is! Your child will eventually learn that having a tantrum does not help him to achieve his goal, in this case the chocolate. As with all 'bad' behaviours, ignore it if possible and instead focus on praising him when he is good.

Your child may need some time to calm down once he has started a tantrum: once he starts it can be difficult to stop and control the storm of emotions that he is feeling. You ignoring the behaviour may be enough for him to calm down, or he may need some help. For example, give him a timeline in which to stop: 'I would like you to stop screaming now: I'm going to count to five and you will stop'. If he does stop, then give him plenty of praise for listening to you. If it is not possible to ignore the behaviour, for example if he is hurting someone else or putting himself in a dangerous position, then remove him for a time out (for example, move him to another room to calm down for a few minutes). In order to deal with a tantrum calmly, you may need to give yourself a time out: step outside to take a few breaths or count to ten.

Once it is all over, try talking to your child about what happened, empathise with him, 'I could see you were very cross with Mummy'; and if you know why the tantrum started, then explain it to him: 'You were cross with Mummy because she wouldn't let you put paint on the carpet'. The explanation helps him to learn to match words with his emotions. This may help him to be able to explain his feelings in the future, and eventually he will be able to have a discussion without the tantrum. Once the tantrum is over, it is done: do not repeatedly refer to his bad behaviour or the tantrum, especially because he is likely to be feeling in need of reassurance, that he is still loved, that you are still there for him – offer him a cuddle. Keep praising the good behaviour and ignoring the bad and with time, as his language skills and emotional maturity develop, the tantrums will gradually stop.

Aggressive behaviour

Aggressive behaviour encompasses fighting, hitting, biting, hair pulling, snatching, pinching and kicking: the scenario in playgroup or the park whereby your child hits another in the sandpit, or your child is the one who is hit. It is common at about the same age as tantrums, approximately 18 months to 3 years old, as your child battles to deal with his emotions, desires and increasing independence but does not yet have the language skills to discuss his wants and needs. Showing this aggressive behaviour does not mean that your child is a bully. Bullying involves persistent attacks on another child, be they verbal or physical, which are designed to hurt. This is generally not the case with a very young child, who is simply lashing out in frustration or experiencing his own hurt.

As with tantrums, watch out for recurrent triggers: if your child is more likely to be aggressive when he is hungry, tired or thirsty, then these outbursts may be preventable. If the behaviour is related to sharing, then encourage turn-taking games. Model good behaviour for your child, so do not show aggression towards him, or even in general when you are cross or frustrated. Your very young child is not yet able to empathise with others, so at 18 months old he may not be able to say how he would feel if someone were to bite him. However, he will understand that his action has a consequence. For example if he bites a child who is on the roundabout because he wants to get on, take him away from the roundabout and explain what you are doing and why. As your child gets older he will be better able to consider other people's points of view. For your 4-year-old it is therefore worth discussing how throwing a ball at another child may make him feel or how he would feel if the ball were thrown at him. Be clear about what is acceptable behaviour and what is not and try to be consistent and calm. For example, if you have told him that pulling hair leads to a time out, then be consistent – even if there are five time outs in a row as he tests the process. Everyone caring for him should follow the same plan, so if you feel that biting needs a time out, agree this with your partner, nursery or any other caregiver. You can try giving your child alternatives; for example, if he wants to snatch or kick, he should try running up and down the room three times and then sit down again. Be sure to keep praising good behaviour, focusing on the good rather than the negative.

Interrupting

'Mummy … Mummy … MUMMY!' It is extremely common for your young child to interrupt all the time; when you are on the telephone or talking to someone else. Yet if you do respond to his interruption, the burning issue which could not wait is likely to be something inconsequential, such as 'I'm going to use the blue paint now'. At around 2 to 3 years old, your child will interrupt continually because he does not understand that the world does not revolve solely around him, and that you are not there only to provide attention and meet his needs. He does not yet have enough of a concept of time to wait for prolonged periods, and as his short-term memory is not fully developed, he may well forget what he has to say if he has to wait. This leads to an urgency to tell you something *now*: he is not aware that interrupting is rude and frustrating – he simply is not yet able to wait! However, this does improve with age, as he becomes better able to wait his turn.

There are some things that you can do to help him to learn not to interrupt. First, model the behaviour that you want him to show, so do not interrupt him, and if you do, apologise for interrupting. Use role play or books to practise not interrupting but also discuss when it is appropriate to do so, for example in an emergency or if he has hurt himself. If you are on a telephone call and he interrupts, do not tell him off and then answer his question or listen to his sentence anyway. This will only teach him that interrupting works, even though he gets told off as well. Instead, acknowledge him, 'I see and hear you, I am just talking for 5 minutes and then I will play with you'; perhaps set the timer so he knows that when it rings you will be finished (though remember that 1 minute is a long time for a 2-year-old!). You could teach him an alternative to interrupting you by calling your name, such as tapping your knee or squeezing your hand and then you respond by a similar signal so that he knows that you are aware of him. Distraction can also work; while you make a telephone call, he could play with stickers, do some colouring or another activity that he can do while being close to you.

Fussy eating

Generally starting at approximately 2 years old, your child will most probably go through a stage of being a fussy eater, where the amount of different foods that he will eat decreases and you may notice that he is eating only a very limited range of foods. This is a part of normal childhood development and is due to 'neophobia' (a fear of new things). As a baby, he probably opened his mouth to everything from fish to beetroot, but he also put non-foodstuffs in his mouth. As your baby gets older and more independent, he begins to learn that it is not safe to put everything in his mouth, that some things may hurt him and that some things definitely taste bad! This means that he only wants to eat things which he recognises as familiar and knows that he likes, as a safety mechanism to stop him eating something new which may or may not be safe. For example, even if he ate bananas 2 weeks ago, if he does not have them again for a while they may seem like a new food and hence he rejects them. Also remember that tastes do change: one day he may like something and the next not!

Here are some tips to encourage your child to eat a varied diet.

- Eat as a family: let him watch you eating new and different foods so he can eventually follow by example. Try to avoid showing dislike of any food yourself, as he is likely to copy! Everyone can eat the same food; you do not need to make him special dinners, but be sure that there is something that he will eat willingly alongside any new foods on his plate.

- Present a new food repeatedly: although it seems a lot, he may need to be offered a new food 10 to 15 times before he decides that he likes it and is willing to eat it.
- Offer new foods in very small amounts: even one bite of a new food should lead to lots of praise.
- Introduce new foods very slowly: start by putting a very small amount of the new food next to foods that he likes on his plate. Praise him for letting you do so. Repeat this the next day, but now draw attention to the new food by asking him about it (its colour, for example). The next day perhaps he could feel it, then smell it, then lick it and eventually eat it. At each stage, lavish him with praise for his actions with the new food, but also for good behaviour, table manners and eating the other food on his plate.
- Take dislikes into consideration: for example, if he prefers crunchy foods, then give raw carrots, before introducing lightly steamed carrots (still with some bite to them), and then softer cooked carrots. Conversely, make a softer food fun; for example, give sticks of vegetables to scoop up mash or a breadstick to dip into hummus.
- Make food fun: and involve him in the preparation of the meal (perhaps he could create a rainbow fruit kebab). Let him go shopping with you and pick a food to make and try.
- Do not force him to eat: whether it is one more bite or the first taste, forcing him to eat may make him start to dread meals.
- Avoid recriminations: do not punish him for not eating. Instead, focus on praise and rewards (such as a small sticker) for trying something new!
- Limit your anxiety: he will pick up on your concerns about food. If mealtimes are a battlefield, you may both be focusing more attention and energy on the battle rather than on the eating itself. Instead, focus attention on good behaviour and conversation at the table: meals are a social activity as well as a method of fuelling up!

Current NHS guidance suggests that all children from 6 months old should be given a vitamin supplement containing vitamins A, C and D, which are vitamins that may need supplementing, especially for a fussy eater. Children's vitamin supplements are available over the counter at a chemist and if you qualify for the Healthy Start scheme, they are available without charge.

Refusing to eat

Another common concern that a parent has is that not only is their child not eating a variety of food, but he does not appear to be eating very much, sometimes less than he did when he was a little toddler. However, this is not a cause for concern because he is not growing as fast as he was in the first year or so of life, so he simply does not need the calories. Your child will be able to self-regulate his appetite and will eat when he is hungry.

Encourage your child's healthy eating with the following tips.

- Do not offer continual snacks: eating between meals will stunt his appetite when it is a mealtime.
- Boycott filling (and sugary) juices: offer water instead.
- Limit the food on his plate: if you put huge amounts of food on his plate, he be overwhelmed when he feels that he will never be able to finish. Put small servings which can be topped up if required.
- Encourage physical activity: this will make sure that he is hungry at mealtimes.
- Avoid urging him to eat: 'just one more (bite)' will lead to stalemate battles as he tries to assert his independence.
- Stop offering snacks directly after a meal: although you may be concerned that he has not eaten enough, he will quickly learn to wait in order to get breadsticks instead of his main meal!
- Look at the larger picture: he meets his nutritional needs over a longer period than one meal, so that one day he may eat very little but the next day he will eat everything!

As long as your child does not appear unwell, but is growing and continuing to develop through play, do not worry about the volume of food he is eating because he will be regulating his own appetite.

Bad language

A young child learns his language by copying, so if he hears swearing and cursing from the adults around him, he is more likely to use those words. He picks up not only the words themselves but their meanings and when they are used from your facial expressions and actions as you say the words. When learning to talk, he may also say a swear word by mistake as he mispronounces another word. Before you can deal with what you find acceptable for your child to say, you need to discuss with your partner which words are acceptable in your house in general. It is confusing for your child if his parents are allowed to use certain language but he is not. So if you do not want your child to copy you, do not swear! However, your child is still likely to pick up bad language, overhearing it in the street or from other children in playgroup, nursery or school. Your child repeating a word he has heard, or asking you what it means, is not the same as him swearing at you. He will notice your reaction when he says a particular word, so if you smile or laugh he is likely to repeat it to make you smile again! Conversely, an extremely negative response may also make him want to repeat the word again, to obtain a similar reaction. An explanation of a swear word is likely to involve concepts that your child may not yet understand. Instead, calmly explain that you do not use such words in your house and be very matter of fact about it. Explain that such words are disrespectful and are not allowed at home, nursery, school or other environments.

If your child has not heard or learnt swear words, he may use toilet humour, or potty talk, instead, such as 'poo poo head' or 'wee wee face'. This can also be to provoke a reaction, albeit a negative one – negative attention is still attention. Again, ignoring the inappropriate behaviour is a good way of defusing it: if it gets absolutely no attention, it is likely to stop. However, if your child is using this language as a taunt to other children, such as 'You are a poo-bum', it may be worth having a quiet and calm conversation asking him how he would feel if someone called him the same name and explaining that we do not call names, or use such words, even if other children are doing so. Giving fun alternatives can also help, so substitute the unacceptable word with a made up one, such as 'shazam' or 'blooglebear'.

Sharing

Your child will find sharing difficult: in fact, many older children and even adults still struggle with the concept of sharing! Your 2-year-old does not have any real idea about sharing or why he should do it. He is not yet able to take someone else's feelings into consideration and does not even understand the whole concept of ownership. This means that he can get frustrated or upset about continual requests to share and may snatch, hit or become distressed if someone takes a toy or if he is forced to share. The first steps towards sharing come when he shows you something that he is playing with or making, but will not let you share it. At about 3 years old, he begins to become aware that not everything belongs to him exclusively and so although sharing remains difficult ('it isn't mine but I want it'), it starts to become easier to explain: 'That is not yours, you'll have to wait your turn'. As your child becomes better at sharing, you may notice that he is better at sharing the toys in nursery or playgroup but not at home because he realises that the toys at nursery are not his, but feels very territorial over the ones at home. As he develops further you will see that he becomes better at sharing, turn taking and playing collaboratively.

Even when your child is too young to understand the concept of sharing, it does not mean that inappropriate behaviour should be ignored. If your child snatches or hits, you need to explain firmly that hitting is not acceptable, at the same time as empathising with him ('I understand that you're upset as you want the toy but we do not hit'). Then introduce the concept of taking turns: that it is someone else's turn and he will be able to have his turn in 2 minutes. If he is the child from whom others snatch his toys, you can teach him the concept of saying no: that it is his turn now. Show him that you are able to share and take turns and explain that you are doing so as you do it, for example if you are cutting up fruit to share. Turn-taking games can help, for example taking turns to mix ingredients in a bowl, to put puzzle pieces in a puzzle or to put blocks away. Role play with soft toys and reading books about sharing can also help reinforce the concept. If you are having a playdate, you can make sharing easier by allowing your child to put away his most special toys, or sometimes his newest toy and prized possession, while underlining the fact that all the other toys are for sharing. Give plenty of praise for good turn taking and sharing and remember that sharing takes time and practice!

Bad manners

The rules of etiquette are many and complex and it is reasonable that your child will not suddenly know and follow the rules of good manners. What is acceptable also varies with age, so you may be thrilled that your 7-month-old picks up his food with his hands but not be impressed if your 4-year-old continues to do so. Yet these rules are complicated for a young child: if you eat cereal with a spoon, why do you eat toast with your hands and not a fork? In the first instance you need to decide what is socially and culturally acceptable in your own home; for example, eating with your hands is perfectly acceptable in some cultures (for example, using a flatbread to pick up the food). You may choose to ignore certain rules of etiquette, for example elbows on the table may not bother you but you do mind if your child wipes his nose on his sleeve.

Your child can be taught 'please' and 'thank you' from an extremely young age. However, instead of asking him 'What do you say?' or telling him off for not saying please, model the behaviour back to him. So when he says 'Want drink', you repeat 'I would like a drink please' and eventually he will copy! Show him what you expect: for example, to wipe his hands on a napkin instead of his trousers or to wipe his nose on a tissue instead of his sleeve. Try to pitch your expectations to the age and development of your child. A 2-year-old is likely to be a messy eater and will not have control over burps or farts; however, if you do not want to encourage burping or farting, avoid laughing or making a fuss over them: instead, simply ignore them and concentrate on praising good behaviour. Be consistent and remember that it will take time!

Nose picking

Nose picking is a common complaint: your child may pick his nose, probably simply because his nose is there, there are holes to stick fingers up and sometimes something interesting to pull out. He may then smell it, lick it or even eat it: he does not mean to disgust you, but rather to explore what he has pulled out! Your child is also likely to pick his nose if it feels bunged up or something is pulling his attention towards his nose when normally it does not bother him at all. So if your child has a cold or an allergy such as hay fever, he is more likely to start nose picking. Once the snot begins to become crusty, it can irritate, so he picks even more. Apart from not being socially acceptable, using dirty fingers to pick can cause infections in the skin of the nose.

In order to prevent nose picking, be sure to treat any allergies (if possible). When he has a cold, give him plenty of fluids to keep the mucous in the nose moist, and if his nose is getting crusty, applying a little of a product such as Vaseline™ to the nostrils can help keep the crusts soft and thus prevent picking. Keep his nails short and encourage hand washing after he goes to the toilet and after mucky activities such as playing in the garden or arts and crafts.

If he is a nose picker, then just as with any other behaviour that you want to change, simply ignore it. Paying attention to it, even if only negative attention, can further encourage the behaviour. Instead, explain that he should not pick his nose and give him a tissue. Give plenty of praise for good behaviour when he uses his tissue. Sometimes making it extreme to the extent that it is really silly can help. For example, pretend that a person on the bus pulled out such a big bogey that it squashed everyone on the bus so that next time he should do it in private or blow his nose on a tissue instead. Your child may be picking just for something to do with his hands, so offer an alternative such as a toy to play with.

Playing with genitals

You may notice that as soon as you take off your child's nappy, their hands are straight down into their crotch to touch their genitals. Both girls and boys may do this. Whilst they are still in nappies this may only be obvious at nappy-changing or bath time, but once they are potty trained it can seem like their hands are always in their pants. They do this simply because it feels good, not in a sexual manner, in that they are not aware of arousal, rather that it feels nice so they keep doing it. As they get older you may notice that they spend a lot of time talking about genitals or even comparing them with friends as they go to the toilet at nursery. Both boys and girls do this and again it is not sexual in nature, they are simply curious about their bodies and the differences between themselves. For example, you may be asked why girls sit down to go to the toilet and boys stand up.

Try to avoid getting into a battle about not touching, or telling them off or punishing for touching themselves, because this may lead to feelings of self-disgust later in life. There is nothing 'wrong' with touching and genitals are not 'bad'; however, you may wish to teach that it is something that you do in private in your room. As with all behaviours that you wish to change, ignore it and focus on praising other behaviour instead. Distraction can also work for young toddlers touching themselves. You can teach your child 'The Underwear Rule' from the NSPCC (National Society for the Prevention of Cruelty to Children): your body is your own and your private parts (the bits under your underwear) are private; no-one should ask to see or touch them there. Caregivers, doctors or nurses may sometimes have to look, but should always explain why first.

Getting rid of a dummy

Your baby may be comforted by the use of a dummy. However, many parents have concerns about the best time to take the dummy away and how to take it away with the least distress. At approximately 6 to 9 months old your baby will begin to develop the idea of object permanence (the idea that things exist even if he cannot see them), so taking the dummy away before that age should be relatively easy: if it is not there, then it does not exist. Once your baby has the concept that things exist even when they cannot be seen, removing the dummy can be more difficult.

A method to help your toddler give up the dummy includes a gradual removal, when you limit the time that he uses the dummy, perhaps for nap times only. You can then give small rewards (such as a sticker on a reward chart) if he manages to have a nap without the dummy. Distract your toddler with exciting games or fun if he asks for his dummy at other times: the aim being that he sees time without his dummy as more exciting and stimulating than time with it. Another technique is to go 'cold turkey' and simply take the dummy away, or give it to the 'dummy fairy' in exchange for another gift, again combining this method with rewards and praise for good behaviour. As with any new situation, reading books about the issue, and role playing giving up the dummy with his toys, can help explain and reinforce the process.

Ignoring/disobeying

It can feel like your child is always ignoring you, disobeying you when you ask him to do something and continually answering with 'no' or 'I won't'. Even your baby at 9 to 12 months old, who is beginning to understand the concept of 'no' or 'don't do that', will often appear to ignore you. Yet he is not being defiant; he simply does not understand why you are saying no. For example, he wants to stick his fingers in a plug socket because he is not aware of any danger and is intent on exploring the world around him. He does not yet have an understanding that he should listen to you, that you are trying to protect and teach him. As a consequence, if he is told off, he does not understand why: though he does understand your tone and facial expression and may get upset. You will therefore need to explain, over and over and over, that he cannot do it, and give him an explanation as to why not. Be consistent with your limits to help your child learn (with lots of practice) what is acceptable and what is not.

As your child gets older you will notice that he may ignore your requests, for example, to stop playing and come for dinner. Again, he is not being defiant; instead he is simply too interested in playing, exploring and becoming independent to obey you. When he is old enough to understand that he needs to follow your instructions, he may still struggle with his desire to do something else, as well as not being able to reason that he could do it later. These conflicting emotions can be confusing and lead to tantrums. Giving time-sensitive warnings in a calm manner can help, for example 'When you have finished your puzzle, it's time to come for dinner'.

As he exerts his independence you may notice that he objects to everything from getting dressed to getting in the car, saying 'no' and refusing to cooperate. Here the need to exert his independence is showing, but he will also be battling between his conflicting desires of dependence, reassurance and independence – his desires to explore the world, the difficulty of controlling his emotions and the need for reassurance from you. Empathise with him: show and tell him that you understand that he is frustrated about coming for dinner but that he can finish playing afterwards and it is time to eat now.

Allow him to make some small decisions. For example, if he is refusing to put away his toys, ask him to choose whether to put away the blocks or the puzzle first, thus removing the choice of whether or not to put the toys away but giving him the choice of which to tidy first. Too much choice is overwhelming, so if you are allowing him to choose his T-shirt for the day, give him a choice of only two. Pick your battles: if it does not matter that he wants to wear two T-shirts, one on top of the other, one day, then allow him to do so! Making some choices can help boost his confidence and self-esteem.

Despite his needs to be independent, he will still be extremely keen to please and help you, so continue to praise good behaviour. Set clear limits about what is acceptable and be consistent with these. As your child gets older you may feel that you have used the word 'no' so often that it has become meaningless – indeed your child will start to ignore you if you are always saying no or shouting. Change what you say from a negative ('No, don't shout') to a neutral or positive statement ('Let's try talking quietly together'), and thus save 'no' for more serious situations.

Lying

Under the age of 3 or 4 years, your child may lie or tell fibs. However, this is not being done with any malicious intent; rather it is that the lines between reality and fantasy are blurred. To him, playing with his imaginary friend or flying to the moon, although fantasy, are a real possibility. So when he tells you that he flew in a rocket today, he is not trying to lie or mislead you: for him, that is what he did, albeit in his imagination.

Your child is also extremely eager to please you, which may encourage wishful thinking. For example, if he snatches a toy from another child and knows that he is not supposed to do this, he may tell you that the other child gave it to him. He is not meaning to lie to you, but rather he wants this to have been the case, and he wants to receive praise for good behaviour. However, this also means that he may refuse to confess when he has done something wrong as he does not want to be told off. Focus on what you do know to be true: 'The saucepans are all out of the cupboard and on the floor', as opposed to 'Did you pull all the pans out and leave a mess?'. Praise him for good behaviour when he does tell the truth – though point out that this does not mean that his previous action does not have a consequence: although you are proud of him for telling the truth, he is not allowed to take everything out of the kitchen cupboards and leave a mess. Model telling the truth for him: try to keep your promises and if you break a promise, tell him and apologise!

Head banging

Between the ages of 18 and 24 months, your child may head bang and this can continue until he is about 3 or 4 years old. It is common: up to approximately 1 in 5 children head bang and it can start as early as 6 to 9 months old. Alternatives to head banging include head rolling or body rocking. Many parents are concerned that their child's head banging is a sign of autism, or another developmental condition, but head banging as a symptom on its own is often part of normal development. A child with a developmental condition such as autism may head bang, but this would be one sign of many other symptoms that are causing concern, such as no or limited eye contact. However, if you are concerned about your child's head banging, see your doctor.

You may notice that your child bangs his head, or rocks rhythmically, before going to sleep and it is thought that this rhythmic behaviour is a way to self-soothe or relax before sleeping, or even to self-soothe during a tantrum. When your baby was in the womb he was rhythmically rocked by the motion of your body, and your baby loves to be held and rocked in the outside world (as do children and adults when they enjoy the swings or fairground rides). The process is self-regulating in that your child is unlikely to continue hitting himself until it hurts: he uses it to self-soothe, not to cause pain. Your child may also head bang as a pain-distraction technique, for example if he has earache or is teething. If head banging brings lots of positive attention from you, then he may head bang to encourage more cuddles!

You can help to protect your child from accidental injury by covering any sharp screws or edges. For example, if he always head bangs in his cot use cot bumpers (soft fabric covering the hard wooden struts of a cot). Do not give attention (even the negative attention of a telling off) to the head banging, and continue to praise his good behaviour. Encourage and stimulate his sense of rhythm during the daytime with marching games or banging instruments. Try alternative soothing routines to wind down before sleep; a warm bath or a cuddle in a rocking chair can help him to relax while also continuing to give some rhythmical stimulation.

Stealing

Your young child does not have a concept of possession, so does not understand that he cannot take things that he wants. Even when he begins to understand that something is 'mine', towards the end of the second year, he still does not understand that not everything can be his. If your child takes something from a shop, he is not trying to 'steal' it; rather, he does not understand that you have to pay for things in a shop. If he takes something from a friend, he does not as yet understand that it does not become his simply because he wants it to!

The rules are difficult to understand: for example, you can bring home a picture that you made in nursery but not a toy, you can bring home a pine cone you found in the street but not someone else's scooter, and you can take a free magazine in a shop but not a packet of crisps. It is understandably confusing for your child. If you notice that your child has taken something, calmly explain why he should not and go with him to take the object back to where it came from. Be consistent and, as always, praise other good behaviour.

Smearing

Smearing is when your child plays with his poo, often smearing it over himself, his clothes or even the walls. He does this because it is interesting: he made it, it is warm, it feels soft, it makes a fantastic mark on the walls or his clothes and it has a smell! Smearing usually starts from approximately 18 months old and can continue until he is about 3 or 4 years old. It often starts when he notices his poo at potty training: 'I made that, ooh what is it?'. Although you may find it revolting, it is usually a normal part of development. However, if it occurs with other symptoms such as no eye contact, it can be one of the signs of autism, or other developmental conditions, so if you have a concern, see your doctor.

If you find your child and his room covered in poo, then, hard as it may be, try not to show any disgust or tell him off. Rewarding him for smearing, be it in a negative way by telling him off, or in a positive way by a nice long warm bubble bath followed by lots of cuddles, may further reinforce the behaviour. Instead, quickly clean him (and the room) without paying lots of attention to the behaviour. You can try to limit his access to his nappy, for example if it tends to occur at nap time, pop him in an all-in-one babygrow or onesie and put it on backwards so he cannot open it.

Smearing could also be a sign that he may be ready to start potty training. When he does a poo on the potty or toilet, give plenty of praise and also allow him an opportunity to have a look if he is interested. Explain what it is and that he can look but should not touch. Continue to praise him for other good behaviour and give him plenty of sensory opportunities to play with clay, finger paints or outside in the mud so that he learns when it is acceptable to make a mess and when it is not. Then clear up together – washing up the paints can be as much fun as the painting itself!

Running away

The moment that you take your child out of the car or buggy, he runs off! This can occur as soon as he is able to walk and it is simply a sign of his excitement and curiosity to explore his environment, without him being aware of any potential dangers. First, talk to him and tell him what you want him to do: 'I would like you to hold my hand while we walk to the park' or 'I would like you to hold on to the car door while I get the coats out'. He may need reminding or it may be easier to turn it into a game, such as doing funny walks or marching as you walk hand in hand. Other games include asking him to help push the buggy or to hold your hand so he can tell you where to go. If you do need him to stop, then tell him exactly what to stop because otherwise he may wonder if he is to stop singing, swinging his arms or looking at the trees. Give a specific instruction: 'Stop running' or 'Stay on the pavement'. Also give him opportunities to run and be independent where appropriate, for example, at the park let him run as long as he is safe and you can see him, giving him the freedom to explore without constraint. If you are not always calling him back you may notice that he stops to check where you are and if he feels he is going too far he will come back on his own. Play games encouraging him to chase you, or run races. If you are going to a crowded environment it may be safer and easier for him to be in the buggy for a period of time.

There has been some debate over the use of toddler reins or harnesses, with some parents finding them helpful and others opposing their use. If you do use toddler reins then be sure to still communicate verbally with your child, telling him how you would like him to behave, without using the reins to physically stop him.

Sibling rivalry

Sibling rivalry is extremely common; after all, why would you not be jealous if you had the sole attention of your parents for a number of years and then someone else came along and asked you to share them? For further information about helping your child to deal with the birth of a sibling, see Chapter 13. As your children get older it is very likely that they will fall out and fight, or swing between playing nicely together, or even adoring each other, and squabbling, fighting and jostling for your attention. Depending on their ages, this fighting may be related to a young child's difficulty with sharing, or a 4-year-old may be very frustrated when his younger sibling keeps knocking down his intricately built brick tower.

As with any behaviour that you wish to change, focus on praising the good times, when your children are playing nicely together and being considerate of each other. Ignore the negative behaviour: do not reward it with attention, albeit of the negative kind. Ignoring the bad behaviour also gives your children an opportunity to sort things out between themselves. If one child is hurting the other, or you feel that the behaviour cannot be ignored, use a time out scenario to remove him until he calms down. Not everything has to be shared equally, including your time. For example, a young baby will inevitably need a lot of your time, but you can discuss this with an older child: as long as he is also given some quality time with you by himself, he can cope with some inequality. Show your children how you want them to behave in a conflict: when you are having a disagreement with your partner, show them that you try to speak calmly to each other.

Breath holding

Breath-holding attacks or spells can start as early as 6 months old, but tend to start in the second year of life. If your child has breath-holding attacks he will probably have grown out of them by the time he is about 6 years of age. They are quite common, occurring in 5%, or 1 in every 20 children. Breath-holding attacks generally start when your child is crying because he is upset or angry: for example, during a tantrum, or if he is hurt after falling or has had a fright. When your child cries and then holds his breath, it can be extremely frightening and distressing for you.

There are two types of breath-holding attacks.

- Blue breath-holding attacks (also called 'cyanotic breath holding'): this is the most common type of breath-holding attack. Here, he starts to cry, often turning red at first before holding his breath and turning blue. The blueness is often most noticeable around his mouth. Very shortly afterwards he may fall to the ground and pass out, or go limp, but after this he will breathe normally and will recover very quickly, within approximately 15 seconds (though it can feel like longer).
- White or pale breath-holding attacks (also called 'pallid breath holding'): this is a rarer type of breath-holding attack. Again, the

attack starts after he is upset, hurt or frightened but here he opens his mouth as if he is going to cry but no sound comes out, before going white and falling to the ground limply. He will come round quickly but may be drowsy for a little while afterwards.

In either breath-holding attack, your child may have a seizure (though this happens rarely). This does not mean that he has epilepsy. The cause of these attacks is not known, though sometimes there is a family history of similar episodes. The attacks are brought on by strong emotions such as upset, frustration, fear or pain and involve the breathing pattern changing as described above, and when your child faints the heart rate and breathing pattern return to normal.

You may be able to prevent breath-holding attacks by distracting your child when he is getting upset, for example by doing a funny dance or singing a silly song. If your child does have a breath-holding attack, lay him on his side and keep a close eye on him. Remove anything from around him on which he may hurt himself when he falls and do *not* put anything, including your fingers, in his mouth. Since the breath-holding attack is not within his control, treat him as normal after the attack. It is not helpful to either punish or reward your child.

After the first attack, it is important to see your doctor as your child will need to be examined for alternative causes for the attack, such as an irregular heartbeat. However, be reassured that no physical cause is usually found for the breath-holding attacks. Breath-holding attacks are not a sign of epilepsy, but if your child has seizures after or during an attack, or if they begin to occur extremely frequently, then you should also see your doctor.

Teeth grinding

Teeth grinding (called 'bruxism') is when your child gnashes or grinds his teeth together, or clenches his jaw together, generally during his sleep. Up to about 4 out of 10 children grind their teeth. It often starts after 3 years old and sometimes stops by 6 years old, though children and adults of all ages grind their teeth! It sometimes starts as early as 6 months of age, when the first teeth come in.

Teeth grinding can be related to pain, for example when he is teething or has earache; it can occur because the top and bottom teeth are not aligned properly; or it can be related to stress. Your child is more likely to grind his teeth if there is a family history of teeth grinding. The sounds that are made by teeth grinding can be pretty loud but in general it does not cause any major problems. You should mention it to your dentist when your child goes for his check-ups so that the dentist can check the teeth thoroughly.

Screen time: television and the internet

Your child may have access to a wide range of screens: televisions, computers, tablets, games consoles and mobile phones. Time spent watching or playing any of these systems adds up to the total screen time that your child has been exposed to over the course of a day, and remember that he may also have exposure during nursery time. So how much is too much?

In the UK, there is currently no official guidance as to how much time a young child should or should not spend in front of a screen. However, it is known that too much screen time, which is essentially a sedentary activity, impacts on the amount of physical activity that your child will have across a day and so can increase the chance of obesity (as does snacking in front of the television!). Too much screen time can also interfere with sleep patterns and can increase the risk of problems such as anxiety and attention issues. Even having the screen on in the background can interfere with your child's concentration. However, this needs to be balanced against the fact that technology is an everyday part of our lives and the fact that your child will need to be able to use such technology.

In the USA, there are guidelines regarding screen time for a child: it is recommended that a child under the age of 2 years has no screen time at all and over the age of 2 years has no more than 2 hours per day. Other countries recommend no screen time for children before the age of 2 years, up to an hour per day for children between the ages of 2 and 5 years, and up to 2 hours after the age of 5 years.

If your child is continually asking for screen time, lead by example and show him that you restrict your own screen time in order to do other activities. Limit the screens to a family area such as the living room (i.e. not in the bedroom) and do not have the television on in the background, for example during mealtimes. Offer alternative games and activities. If your child is old enough, then set limits, for example you can agree with a 4-year-old that he is allowed one half-an-hour programme and so he has to choose between A and B. Watch with your child so that you can talk about the programme together and take the opportunity to discuss what happened and how the characters felt, etc. If your child is playing games on a tablet or computer, taking an interest means that you can not only monitor what he is seeing and playing, but also talk about it with him.

The internet is a fantastic resource, but just as you would not let your young child play in the park unattended, there are methods to keep your child safe on the internet. Use the parental controls that are available on your television, games consoles, computers and tablets to limit what your child can access online. Download age-appropriate apps or games and try them out before he uses them. Talk to your child about the internet and tell him that if he ever sees something that makes him feel worried, or if he is not sure what something does or is, he should stop what he is doing and talk to you about it.

Difficult questions and tricky situations

We all learn by asking questions about the world around us, and you will notice that your child has many, many questions. Some of the more difficult or potentially controversial questions and situations are covered in this chapter. Where appropriate, suggestions as to how to discuss these topics with your child are included. There are no right and wrong answers, and the suggestions given are simply that – suggestions. However, it is worth speaking to your partner or considering how you would like to answer the questions so that you feel prepared!

'Why?'

From approximately 2 years old, you may notice that your child asks questions all the time, and no matter how many answers you give, he will keep asking. For example 'Why are we going shopping?': 'To buy food': 'Why?': 'Because we need food to eat': 'Why?': 'So we don't get hungry': 'Why?': 'Because we need food for energy': 'Why?': and so on, and so on, and so on!

As your child begins to understand that things are related, that we do things for a reason, and that things happen for a reason, he will ask more and more questions because he is interested in the answers. The more he asks, the more he is learning! So, as much as it can try your patience sometimes, it is important to stay calm and answer as many of his questions as you can. And if you do not know the answer, then tell him that you do not know, but then give him (and yourself) a tool to find out the answer later. For example, 'Let's go and look for a book in the library about . . .'. Try asking him what he thinks the answer is; this can be useful as your child gets older, encouraging him to think for himself. No question or answer is stupid or wrong because they all lead to learning!

'Where do babies come from?'

This question often first appears if you are pregnant with a sibling for your child, or if a relative or friend is pregnant. As with all questions, the answer is dependent on the age of your child: a 3-year-old is unlikely to understand, and does not really need to know, the exact biological details of reproduction, pregnancy and labour! Depending on how much you think your child will understand and how much you want to tell him, you may wish to start with the fact that mummies can grow babies in a special place called a womb which is in their tummies. If he asks how the baby gets there, then you could tell him that mummies have eggs and daddies have seeds, and when the daddy gives his seed to the mummy, the egg can grow in her tummy to make a baby. Again, depending on how many questions your child is asking and whether or not he appears to be satisfied with your responses, you can choose whether or not to continue. Your child may ask for further details, such as 'Where do the seed and egg come from?' and 'How does the daddy give the seed to the mummy?'. Stay calm and try to avoid laughing at your child's questions as he tries to figure out what you are talking about. For example, he may respond to your comment about the daddy having a seed by asking whether he needs to water your tummy because he is using information he knows about seeds in a new context. Be matter of fact: for your child his questions are a fact-finding exercise and as yet he does not have an understanding of the adult emotions around sex and having children. These matter-of-fact conversations open the lines of communication:

telling your child that you are happy to discuss such topics means that it will be easier to keep talking about these issues as your child gets older. Your child may role play being pregnant, or breastfeeding, with dolls. Reading books with your child about having babies and where they come from, as well as about having a new baby brother or sister, can also be useful.

Dealing with a new baby

The first question that tends to arise is when to tell your child that you are expecting. Before you tell him, you may wish to start having some conversations about, or reading books about, having a brother or sister. For example, after he has been playing with a friend who has siblings, you might mention that he might have a brother or sister in the future. A very young child, younger than approximately 18 months, is unlikely to notice that you are pregnant until well into the third trimester when your bump gets big, so there is little benefit in explaining to him earlier than this. The baby is not visible to him, and he has little concept of time, so cannot understand that the baby is coming 'later' or 'soon'. However, if your child is more than 2 years old, you may wish to tell him when you tell other family and friends as they are likely to try to talk to him about it.

Your young child may not react very much at all when you tell him that there is a baby growing inside Mummy and that he will have a brother or sister. Or he may appear excited, upset or confused. As always, give him time and space to tell you how he is feeling and offer lots of cuddles and comfort. If your child is interested, you can encourage this interest by letting him be your helper: telling Grandma the news, or choosing a blanket or muslin for the baby. Your child will love hearing about himself, so show him pictures of himself as a baby and talk about how he was and how you felt when he was born. This is a great opportunity to prepare him for what life will be like when the baby comes, so a picture of him breastfeeding or sleeping is an opportunity to tell him that the baby will not be able to play with him straightaway, will sleep and eat a lot and will cry to get their needs met. Then focus on what he can do with his sibling, for example hold a hand or stroke a foot.

Include your child in your preparations for the baby: he loves to help out and the praise that he receives for doing so, so let him choose a babygrow or help you to fold the baby's washing. If your child needs to move bedroom, or move out of his cot, in order to make space for the baby, try to do this a few months before the baby is born so that he does not feel that the baby has forced him to move. Make the move an exciting event which is special in its own right – a big boy's bed!

You will need to make a plan for when you go into labour and, if your child is old enough to have a concept of time, then explain this to him. For example, warn him that Grandma will look after him that day and that he will come and see you in the hospital. When he does come to the hospital to see you, try to make it at a quiet time, without other visitors, so that he can spend time with you. When he arrives, give him lots of attention: you may wish to allow someone else to hold the new baby so that you can give your child a proper hug before introducing him to the baby. Some parents like to give a gift from the new sibling to the older child, and your older child could make a welcoming gift or card for the new baby. When you introduce him to the baby, it can be helpful to keep referring to your older child, for example 'You had feet this tiny too'.

Just as it will take you time to adjust to the change of a new baby, so it will take time for your older child to adjust. Your child may not appear very interested in the new baby; or be very demanding of attention; or regress in his behaviour in order to get attention (for example, wanting to use a bottle or wear a nappy); or show his feelings by being a bit rough with the baby or the baby's toys. As with any behaviour that you wish to discourage, try to avoid shouting or punishing bad behaviour and focus on praising the good behaviour. Set your boundaries very clearly: for example, if your older child hits the baby then be very clear that this is not acceptable and will lead to a time out or other consequence. Giving your older child jobs such as holding the towel for you when you get the baby out of the bath or gently stroking baby's back after a feed can help to make him feel involved with his new sibling. Even just asking his opinion, for example asking him whether he thinks the baby should use the white blanket today or the blue one, makes him feel like a good helper, and so you can give him some attention and lots of praise!

Read books about new siblings and give your child opportunities to role play looking after his own baby doll. Give him space to talk to you about how he feels and do not worry if he tells you that he does not like the baby because he probably means that he does not like the changes that the baby has made in his life, not the actual baby. Also, do not worry if he does not seem at all interested!

Try to give your child special time alone with you: this does not have to be long; perhaps he will go to bed at night 10 minutes after the baby, or during the baby's nap time. He now gets to have your undivided attention to do whatever he wants: read a story, play a game or just have a snuggle. During the course of the day, give him reminders that this time is coming up later and that you are looking forward to it, and afterwards tell him how much you enjoyed your special time and are looking forward to it tomorrow. Most importantly, give him, and yourself, time to become used to the new family unit!

Explaining the death of a grandparent or pet

Your child will have some awareness of death, even before it truly encroaches on his life, either through books, or passing a dead bird in the street, or a squashed insect in the garden. However, he does not have a true understanding of the permanence of death and the feelings that accompany the loss of a loved one. It is probable that your child will experience the death of someone or something close to them at a young age, be it a grandparent, other relative or a pet; and you will need to be able to talk to him about this situation.

As with all conversations, how much your child understands will depend on his age. Children are very practical and so an approach explaining that Grandma's body stopped working, that she could not eat or breathe or go to the toilet, may be useful. Some parents may describe death as going to sleep or not waking up from a sleep, but this may not be helpful as your child may take it literally and become anxious about going to bed, or you going to bed, at night. He will have difficulty understanding that death is permanent and may ask repeatedly when Grandma is going to come back, so you may have to repeat the conversation many times. If you have a faith you may find it helpful to refer to this during these conversations, so if you believe in heaven then you may want to discuss this with your child.

Your child may respond to death by becoming clingy or anxious, or he may appear to have no reaction at all, which is also normal. He may ask repeated questions or act out his feelings and the situation with role play (for example, playing dead or playing at being sad). He may be more distressed by the sadness of the people around him rather than for himself. Again, books can help to give examples and aid discussions about this subject.

Some deaths may affect your child very deeply, for example the loss of a parent, sibling or close friend: if you are concerned about how your child is dealing with such a situation, seek your doctor's advice.

'I hate you!'

It can be a shock when your sweet little baby shouts that he hates you! However, try not to take it personally; he is expressing his emotions about something, just not in a particularly helpful or articulate way! So when you tell him that it is bath time and he is playing with his toys and shouts 'I hate you!', he is not actually saying that he hates you, rather that he hates the fact that he has to stop playing, but he is not quite sure how to get his feelings across. You can help him to put his feelings into words: tell him that you can see that he is cross that he has to finish playing now, but it is bath time. He is trying to translate his big feelings into a word or two: he does not hate you at dinner time because you want him to eat broccoli, but he is frustrated that you want him to do something that he does not want to do! It is important not to show that he has upset you with his words, as this may encourage him to say it again in order to get a response. Instead, show him that you can see that he is angry or upset and give him the space and opportunity to tell you why. When he is struggling with his emotions, offer a simple hug!

'Why doesn't he/she like me?'

It can be extremely upsetting when your child comes home from nursery or school and tells you that he does not have any friends, played alone in the playground, or is sad because someone told him that he does not like him or does not want to be his friend. As a parent your instinct is to protect your child from all pain, be it physical or emotional, and many parents have memories of awkward social situations as children. In the first instance allow your child to express his emotions: do not tell him not to be upset or that he is overreacting – he is upset! Give him time and space to tell you how he is feeling and then you can discuss it. A young child can often be hurtful to another child without realising it, sometimes when he is tired, hungry or just grumpy. Talk about the situation: your child may be upset by a comment that another child made, but give them the opportunity to sort things out for themselves. Often, a hurtful comment or action is forgotten the next day (or even in 5 minutes!). Give your child a coping strategy: 'If you want to play scooters with Ben, you will need to take turns' or 'If Sam doesn't want to play with you then maybe you could play with Alex'. Arrange a playdate at home or in the park: this gives your child an opportunity to play with his friends in another environment, away from nursery. However, if you feel that the situation is more serious or if you feel that it has a negative impact on his desire to go to nursery or school, speak to his teacher.

14

Helping your child at nursery or school

This chapter covers how to help and support your child at nursery and school. 'Nursery' is used to mean a nursery covering the year before Reception entry at school, and not a childcare option that takes your child from a very young age.

The first day

Starting nursery or school is a nerve-wracking experience, not just for your child but also for you as a parent! Your concerns may be varied, such as whether your child will settle in, make friends, eat lunch and how you will cope with the change yourself.

As always, it is important not to communicate your fears and anxieties to your child. Instead, make going to nursery or school an exciting idea and discuss how much you are looking forward to it, what a great time he will have and how many wonderful activities are offered. You can prepare him by discussing that you will take him into nursery but then will have to leave and the teachers will look after him, and then, like always, you will come back to get him. Reading books about nursery and role playing going to nursery can be helpful.

Get organised the night before! Having to rush in the morning trying to get together school uniform, labelling it, packing a PE bag and making a packed lunch (if needed) will add to the stress of the morning, so do as much as you can the night before. Set your alarm to give you enough time to get everyone up, dressed and out of the house having eaten breakfast in a calm, not rushed, manner. Be clear about bedtimes, as it can be hard to persuade a tired child to get out of bed in the morning!

Many schools and nurseries will have a settling-in process in the first few days and weeks of the autumn term. This may involve you coming in with your child for a short amount of time and/or you leaving your child for gradually increasing amounts of time. Your school will explain to you how their process works and will be used to dealing with both nervous parents and children!

Keep talking to your child and reassuring him as needed. Do not be surprised if everything appears to be going well but after a few weeks your child suddenly starts getting upset about going to school. In this situation, the excitement of the first few days is over and he suddenly realises that he is going to have to go to school *every* day and begins to get nervous again.

For you as a parent, watching your child run off happily to line up into the classroom can be just as hard as peeling off a clinging child. Just as your developing child is finding the balance between dependence and independence, you are also adjusting to the same change. The majority of children will settle into school or nursery within a few weeks: if you are having concerns at any point, speak to your child's teacher.

How to encourage your child to tell you about the school day

'What did you do at school today?'

'Nothing.'

It is very common for you to be frustrated when your child refuses to tell you what he did at school, saying that he did not do anything or cannot remember. First, think about the best time to ask him; the journey home from school is often not a great time for talking. Put yourself in his shoes: when you come home from work after a long and busy day you may be tired, hungry (and a bit grumpy), and not particularly willing to talk about what you did all day in great detail! Your child may be more communicative during dinner, bath time or just before bed, even if it is a bedtime stalling technique for a few minutes! Listen out for any conversation openers that your child may give; if he happens to tell you something, use the opportunity to open a conversation.

Your child may respond to general, open questions such as 'How was school?', or he may need more specific questions such as 'Who did you play with at break time?' or 'What was for lunch today?'. Avoid closed questions with yes/no answers such as 'Did you do reading?', because this does not give him an opportunity to give you extra information. He may benefit from you signposting him with time frames to divide his day. He may be too young to be able to tell the time, so asking him what he did at 10.30am will not get an answer, but he may be able to remember the day (or parts of the day) as a sequence of events. For example, ask him: 'What did you do after we hung your coat up and you went into the classroom?'; 'What were you doing before snack time?'; 'What did you play with after lunch?'; and 'Who were you playing with before tidy-up time?'. Giving more structure to your questions may help him to talk to you about his day and hence he gives you more information. Your school may be able to help by talking you through the layout of a typical day or telling you that there is PE or music on a specific day so that you can ask relevant questions. Reading the school newsletter is another opportunity to kick-start a topic of conversation about what happened at school, as is talking about the artwork or other work that he brings home. For an older child, you can use a more open-ended question, such as 'What was the most interesting part of school today?' or 'What was the best and worst part of school today?', to open the lines of communication. Alternatively, once he has started making friends you can ask about specific children at school.

Once he is talking, give him plenty of attention and be interested! Showing that you are a good listener will encourage him to talk, as well as modelling to him the importance of listening well. Make the conversation two way and tell him about your day in return. Remember that he may not always want to talk about his day and that sometimes this is OK!

Making friends and dealing with bullying

Making friends is a challenge for adults and children alike! A young child 'parallel plays', that is, he plays alongside other children, both doing the same activity. As he gets older, he moves on to actually playing with other children. The process of making friends at school or nursery takes time, so do not expect your child to come running home on the first day to tell you about his 'three new best friends', though of course he might!

You can try to help your child by using the class list to talk about children in his class when you are at home. Even knowing one or two names of children in his class can help to start the conversation. Arranging playdates at home or in the park gives him one-to-one time with another child to start building a relationship in a calm environment. It is natural that he may prefer spending time with certain children; no-one likes everyone; so try to accept his friend choices. Your child may need some help with starting conversations or initiating play; here role play is a great way to practise. For example, if he often sees a child that he wants to play with in the sandpit, you could suggest that he asks the child if they can build sandcastles together.

Playing together is an opportunity to keep practising social behaviours, such as sharing, turn taking and losing at a game instead of always winning. You may have noticed that your child is bossy during play and that other children do not like this. If so, try talking to your child, or role playing, in order to show him that he needs to try letting someone else have a turn at being the leader. Show him that you are a good friend, that you are kind and empathetic, so he can copy this in his own relationships.

If your child does tell you about an issue or problem with a friend, do not interrupt with a method to fix it. First, listen and show that you are listening and help your child to identify how he was feeling; for example, 'Were you cross?'. Do not automatically blame either child in a scenario. Second, discuss what happened next, as many situations will have been resolved between the children, with or without the help of school staff, so that your child may simply be reporting the situation as opposed to asking what do to next. However, if your child is stuck, 'She won't play with me', then ask him what he thinks he should do. Give him time to think before offering suggestions yourself as he may well have an answer, for example 'Play with someone/something else'. If he does not have an answer then you can offer some coping mechanisms: give him choices so that he feels in control of the situation. 'You could play with Rob instead', or 'Ask her what she would like to play with after the sandpit, so that you can play together'.

If your child constantly reports a problem with another child and you have concerns, speak to his teacher. Bullying can occur in young children and can take various different forms, ranging from physical aggression to consistently being excluded from play. It is important to try to distinguish between bullying, where there is an intent to hurt someone (either their feelings or physically), and underdeveloped social skills, which are extremely common in young children. Your child's school will have an anti-bullying policy and his teacher will be able to help, so if you are worried, speak out.

Eating at school

Many parents are concerned that their child may not eat school lunches or his packed lunch and may be hungry during the school day. Even if your child has a packed lunch, it may not always be easy to discover what he has (or has not) eaten because food can be swapped or discarded. First ask your child and then ask the teacher! For your young child, lunch-time assistants are often on hand and can monitor his eating. If he is not eating and you are concerned, then ask for information: perhaps your child has not eaten the main course but has had some bread and butter and a piece of fruit, as well as fruit snacks and milk throughout the day. Your child may eat less because he feels rushed, is too busy talking with his friends, or wants to dash outside to play. If he is not eating much, ask the teacher if he appears to be affected in the afternoon (if he is tired or finds it difficult to concentrate). The staff at school may be able to help with all these issues. If your child has packed lunches, get him involved with what he would like to include to encourage him to eat.

If your child does come home from school starving, then have some healthy snacks ready, such as fruit, cheese, yoghurt or a sandwich. He may come home from school and 'catch up' on lunch before eating dinner later on. Try to avoid too many treat foods as your child may learn to wait for these instead of eating lunch. As always with food, encourage and praise good behaviour, rather than focusing on the negatives and what he did not eat. As long as your child is growing and is healthy, he is probably meeting his nutritional needs.

Supporting your child at school

Showing an interest in your child's schooling and learning will help support him at school and will help him to achieve and reach his potential. No matter your own feelings about school, try to be positive for your child, otherwise he may copy your negative emotions.

Give plenty of praise and encouragement for your child's achievements at school, no matter how big or small. Try to focus praise on how well he is trying as opposed to focusing solely on results. This will encourage your child to be a good learner (who will make mistakes) as opposed to discouraging him from trying something new in case he gets it wrong. If your child has homework (at a young age this is likely to be reading), set aside quiet time to do it with him, without the television or other distractions.

Get involved at school: meet his teacher if possible, attend parents' evenings, read the newsletters or volunteer for the school, perhaps to attend an outing, to read with children or to work on the parent–staff association (PSA). The more involved you are, the better informed you will be to help your child.

You can read to your child and sing nursery rhymes and songs from early babyhood. The following section gives some ideas of how to help your older child with literacy (reading and writing) and numeracy. There is no 'set age' as to when you can play these games and activities with your child: it depends on when he is ready. However, many of the games and activities described are aimed at a child in pre-school nursery and Reception (3, 4 and 5 years old): see what you think your child may engage with and find fun. Some of the information given below is a guide as to how your child may be learning during the Reception year at school. Your child's nursery and school may be able to give you further advice and ideas.

Helping with literacy

The term 'literacy' covers many different areas of language, not simply reading. In order to read and write, your child will need to develop language for thinking, to explain his thoughts, and language for communicating (his speech, body language and writing). He needs to be able to link sounds to letters, and conversely letters to the sounds that they make (this is called 'phonics'), in order to read and spell. He will then develop writing and handwriting. Literacy and the ability to communicate thoughts is at the heart of much of school learning, even that of maths and science, where a specific language develops.

There are many activities that you can do with your child to help him develop literacy skills.

Language for thinking and communicating

- Talk to each other: although this sounds obvious, have lots of conversations about whatever subject interests him and you. A good opportunity to do this is at mealtimes. Ask open-ended questions such as 'What did you do?' or 'What did you think/feel about ...?', as opposed to closed questions such as 'Did you play trains?' which will lead to a yes/no answer. Conversation also teaches him the rules of speech (for example, listening to other people, not interrupting, remembering what the other person said and taking turns).

- Use the telephone: let him speak to a relative or a friend, which is a good opportunity to practise turn taking, and also removes the non-verbal forms of speech such as facial expressions and body language.
- Ask about his feelings: this is often easier when linked to specific situations. For example, if he is telling you about a time at school when someone would not share with him, ask him how he felt, which helps him to put language to his emotions.
- Invite solutions to suitable problems: if he will not eat certain vegetables or he wants to watch television after bedtime, ask him what he thinks that you, as a family, should do. Not only does this help with his language skills but it also makes it more likely that he will comply with whatever agreement you come to!
- Role play with puppets or teddies: invent a story, use different voices and get him to play more than one role (so that he experiences the story from different viewpoints, thereby learning to understand that other people have different feelings from his own).
- Play describing games: put different objects (such as a hairbrush, toothbrush or apple) into a bag and blindfold him (or ask him to close his eyes). He then puts a hand into the bag and picks up an object, which he has to describe: does it feel big, round, spiky, smooth, etc. Finally, he guesses what the object is.
- Tell stories from your own childhood: he will love to hear these stories, especially if they have other people he knows in them. The telling of stories portrays the idea that stories have a beginning, middle and end, and the telling of a memory is an example of giving speech or language to a thought.
- Respond with questions: if he asks you 'Why?', try asking 'Why do *you* think?' to encourage him to think about the issue.
- Introduce new words: and give him an explanation as to meaning. For example, you might find 'anxious' in a book, so tell him that it means 'worried' or 'nervous', and then read the phrase again using the new word and one of your explanations. If a word is very familiar for him, throw in a new option at book time (for example, substitute 'huge', 'large', 'gigantic' or 'enormous' for 'big').

- Play memory games: in 'I went to the shop and bought . . .', each person adds an item to the shopping list, and the next person has to recite the whole list of items already said before adding their own item.
- Use a dictionary: if you do not know a word, show him how to find out what it means and help him to use a dictionary.
- Explain your thoughts and actions: tell him why you are doing something or why you are thinking something. For example, 'I'm going to do the laundry now as the clothes are dirty, we don't want to wear smelly clothes and we need fresh ones for the morning'. This helps him to develop the ability to explain his own ideas.

Phonics: linking sounds to letters, leading to reading

Your child learns to read and write by using the sounds which are made by the letters of the alphabet (26 letter sounds), as well as sounds made up by combinations of letters, such as 'ee', 'oo', 'ou', 'sh' and 'ng'. There are 44 sounds in total. Once your child has learnt all the sounds, he learns to read by blending sounds together ('c–a–t' sounds 'cat'), and then learns to spell by segmenting words into their separate sounds.

- Play with letters: using magnetic letters, bath letters or letter stamps, help him to make simple consonant–vowel–consonant words (for example, 'm–a–t').
- Ask him the sounds for the start or end of a word.
- Play I Spy: rather than a starting letter, play with a starting sound (for example, 'I spy with my little eye something that starts with the sound "a" ').
- Make a 'sounds' chart: use either a large piece of paper with pockets made from smaller pieces of paper, a chain of small bags along a piece of string, or a row of empty jars. Label each pocket, bag or jar with a letter. With or without his help, cut out items from magazines or catalogues. Ask him to place the picture in the pocket/bag/jar according to the starting sound. It does not matter if the correct sound does not match with the correct spelling. For example, it is correct if he puts 'giraffe' in the 'j' pocket instead of the 'g' because this is phonetically correct. At this point you are concentrating on the sound as opposed to the correct spelling.
- Introduce active learning: place cards with letters on them around a room or your house, shout out words and ask him to run to the

starting letter sound. Or give him a small basket of items and ask him to place the items on the correct card for the beginning letter.

- Instigate a phonics treasure hunt: pick a letter and hunt for objects around the house that start with the sound. For example: 'b' – bread, banana, butter, bed, bath ...
- Play sound snap: use picture cards and shout 'Snap!' if they start with the same sound.
- Encourage rhyming games: start by giving him a choice ('Does cat rhyme with mat or frog?'); then progress to choosing the odd one out ('Which one doesn't rhyme: cat, mat, frog or hat?'); finally ask 'Can you think of a word which rhymes with cat?'. This can be played with picture cards or without, which is handy for car journeys!
- Ask him to split words into syllables, such as 'fing–ger'.
- Play alphabet lotto: create bingo cards with a small number (perhaps five or six) of pictures of objects on them. Place letter cards or counters face down in the middle. Each person picks a counter and places it on the relevant place on their card if the object starts with the sound of their letter counter. If not, the counter is placed back in the middle. The winner is the first person to cover all their pictures.
- Encourage word play with rhyme and alliteration (the same starting sound): 'The fat cat sat on the mat' or 'silly, smelly, sausages' encourage him to listen for the sounds within words. Leave a gap and ask him to fill it: for example, 'The sausages are silly, slimy and ...?'.
- Use a computer: you can find numerous apps and websites with phonic or letter sound games.

Reading

- Read yourself: show him that you read, both for pleasure and for a purpose. Read a wide variety of items: books, magazines, newspapers, letters, recipes and emails.
- Read together: choose a wide range of books (fiction, non-fiction and poetry).
- Talk about the book itself: discuss how a book is set out (the title, author, illustrator, contents page, chapters, etc.)
- Demonstrate blending: when you are reading together, choose simple consonant–vowel–consonant words and sound them out.
- Look at the pictures: when you have read a book to him, ask him to 'read' it back to you, or to his teddy or doll, by describing the illustrations in the book in his own words.

- Encourage predictions and summaries: when reading a book, stop and ask him 'What do you think will happen next?'. At the end of a book, ask him to summarise what happened. Change the story ending, or ask him to end the story in a different way.
- Practise empathy: ask him why he thinks characters are behaving in a certain way in a book. Act out the story: use different voices and props.
- Make up stories: start with asking him what happens next in the book you are reading; then take turns to create your own story together.
- Ask his opinion: why does he like a particular book? For example, is it the pictures, the front cover, a character, the rhyming of words, the nonsense words or the comedy?
- Read books over and over: hearing the same books and words repeatedly can help with learning sounds. He may not be reading yet but he will notice if you miss something out, or may be able to finish the ends of sentences in the book: point to the words as he says them.
- Read alternately: once he has started to read, perhaps he can read a word or a sentence per page, and you read the rest in order to keep the story moving.
- Keep reading to him: even if he has learnt to read, you can read him books that are more difficult and complex than the words he can read and you can then discuss these together.
- Encourage the use of phonics: sound out words, even those that are completely unfamiliar (for example, the word is not in his school reading book or even in a children's book). Read the words that are all around us: in supermarkets and on road signs, transport timetables or food labels.
- Go to the library: let him choose books for enjoyment, as many and as often as he likes. You are aiming to create a love of reading and books!

Writing

- Encourage mark making on paper: and give meaning to those marks ('What does that say?'). Create marks with a purpose and a meaning; for example, create road signs, town maps and treasure maps together.
- Create big letter shapes: let him use his fingers to make letter shapes in sand, mud and the steam on the bathroom tiles; or he could use a paint roller dipped in water to make marks on the garden fence.

- Use a variety of materials: he can make marks using chalks on paving stones and sticks in mud. He can also make letter shapes with playdough and cooked spaghetti!
- Try dot-to-dots and mazes: start by tracing the line with a finger before using a pencil to try to stay within the lines.
- Demonstrate that writing has a purpose: write a shopping list, a recipe or a note to someone.
- Develop his fine motor skills: handwriting requires control of the fingers and hands, so encourage him to use tweezers, thread beads on a string (or Cheerios™ on a length of liquorice rope!), peg up washing and sort tiny objects.
- Write together: when you write something (for example, a birthday card or a shopping list), ask him to fill in the words he knows.
- Make lists: for example, 'Things I like to play with'.
- Write down a question: for example, 'What did you do today?' or 'What did you eat for lunch?'. Let him respond how he chooses: he could draw a picture or make marks and words with letters.

Helping with numeracy

Maths and numbers surround us: numbers on houses, in recipes, paying for items in shops, even counting out treats to share! Numeracy is more than just numbers; it covers topics such as time, money and shapes. Puzzles, building toys and games can all be great to help with maths.

- Sing! He will not mind (or even notice) if you have a terrible singing voice, so sing away with nursery rhymes and counting and clapping songs and rhymes. For example: '1, 2, 3, 4, 5, once I caught a fish alive'; 'Five little ducks went swimming one day'; '1, 2, buckle my shoe'; 'Ten green bottles'; and 'Ten in a bed'. Use your fingers to give a visual illustration of the numbers as you sing them!
- Read books with numbers: these may be written as figures, in words and/or with pictures representing the numbers (if the text says 'four frogs', there is a picture with four frogs). Numbers could be part of the story. Count the objects in the pictures, pointing to each object in turn, which encourages one-to-one correspondence (meaning that each frog counts as one frog; so you point to the first frog in the picture for number one, and then to the second frog to count to two, etc.).

- Play clapping games: to encourage counting, get him to close his eyes and then you clap a number of times (starting with a small number). Ask him how many claps he heard, or to clap it back to you. Then take turns, using different rhythms.
- Count! Everything and everywhere: the number of stairs up and down, the number of toy cars he tidies up, or the number of jumps it takes to get to the car. Look for numbers together: on houses, letter boxes, number plates, shops or price tags.
- Play Hunt the Number: as he becomes more confident with identifying numbers, ask him to find you a house with a number 4, or a price tag with a number 9.
- Estimate amounts: for example, when you are taking out the box of toy cars, ask him to estimate how many cars there are. Perhaps picking up the box or shaking it may give him a clue. Then take out the cars one at a time, counting them, to see how accurate his estimate was.
- Be silly! When counting, make a mistake and miss out or repeat a number to see if he corrects you. This is a good way to see if he recognises the order in which numbers occur. Try counting onwards from four instead of one, or try counting backwards from ten. As he becomes more confident, try asking questions such as 'What is one more than three?' (and perhaps use a practical example, such as carrot sticks during lunchtime).
- Use real-life examples: the introduction of simple addition and subtraction using practical examples will help him to learn the more abstract ideas when he is older. It is easier to add two packets of chocolate biscuits and one packet of plain biscuits to make three packets of biscuits altogether, than to do the sum $1 + 2 = ?$, especially if the packets themselves are in front of him as he helps you to unpack the shopping!
- Introduce games with a dice: count the dots on the dice and then move your piece the number of spaces on the dice. Or roll the dice and use the number he throws to count on from, or back from: for example if he rolls a 3, count 3, 2, 1 and 3, 4, 5, 6. Or use the dice to determine how many blocks he puts on his tower, or raisins he gets as a treat. As he gets older and more confident with numbers you can make it harder, throwing the dice to collect blocks and the winner is the first person to obtain ten blocks (or go the other way: start with ten blocks and the winner is the first to zero). Dice are a good way of introducing early addition and subtraction: if

you throw two dice and get, for example, a 2 and a 3, you move your counter two places and then a further three, so five places altogether.

- Organise a number treasure hunt: find two toys, three apples, four teddies, etc.; or try collecting groups of numbers – two cups, two plates and two spoons.
- Play ordering games: stick a small numbered sticker onto the bottom of cars, or cut out pictures of animals or toys from a catalogue and place numbered stickers on the back, and ask him to put them in order. Start small scale (numbers 1 to 3) and then increase the scale (1 to 10 or 20). Or you could draw, for example, ladybirds with different numbers of spots and then ask him to put them in order. If he likes a more active form of learning, then you could draw the ladybirds without the numbers, and ask him to stick on dots, or place small balls of playdough to represent the dots. Once they are ordered, take one away and ask him which number is missing; or reverse two numbers and ask him what is wrong and how to fix the number line. Alternatives include pegging small cards with numbers onto a washing line or sticking numbers onto a poster (using Blu-tack™ so they can be removed easily!).
- Make patterns: use everyday objects or toys – one red brick, one yellow, one blue, etc.
- Use practical everyday activities: many activities involve counting, such as setting the table ('How many forks?') or cooking ('How many spoonfuls of flour?'). Paying in a shop introduces money skills.
- Encourage sorting skills: sorting out the washing, by colour or by number, can involve counting (for example how many black socks?). When you pair up the socks, you are sorting into piles of two, and this may be a way of introducing the idea of counting in twos.
- Explore shapes: your baby has enjoyed playing with shape-sorter toys, but do not put them away too early. Your older child may want to have the shape to hold when he is learning about the different qualities of shapes: for example, the number of edges and faces. Use shapes to make patterns: two circles, one square, two circles, etc. Look for shapes in the real world: a jam jar is a cylinder and the television is a rectangle. Play 'I Spy' with shapes: for example 'I spy a circle' when you are looking at a circular cushion.
- Talk about time: with discussions such as 'What time is lunchtime?' and 'How long does bath time take?'.

- Discover size: play games encouraging the language around size (small: smaller: smallest, big: bigger: biggest, short: tall, narrow: wide and more: less). Discuss which container in the bath holds more water, or which box holds the most cars. Line up objects in order of size, weight or height.
- Play Hunt the Object: you hide a toy and tell him where to look with instructions such as 'Take two steps forward, then look *under* the table'. Directional language words include: 'under', 'over', 'through', 'on top of', 'behind', 'in front of', 'next to', 'beside', 'between', 'up' and 'down'. As he becomes more confident, increase the complexity of the instructions that you give. For example: 'Walk between the two chairs, then the toy is on top of the counter next to the fruit bowl and in front of the pen'. Then let him hide a toy and give you instructions to find it.
- Encourage building games: use blocks or linking blocks, such as Duplo™ and Lego™. These are great for counting, designing patterns, building shapes and generally seeing how everything fits together.
- Introduce the concept of division: keep it practical, for example, sharing the number of raisins or apple slices between some friends or between you and him at lunch. This is also a good way of emphasising the importance of sharing!

Appendix

How to make your own playdough and saltdough

Playdough is easily available in many shops and supermarkets but you may find it cheaper to make your own. Saltdough is generally not commercially available as it dries out quickly. There are many recipes for both types of dough readily available. The other advantage of making your own doughs is that you can involve your child in the making process!

Playdough

Ingredients:

1 cup (125g) flour
½ cup (25g) salt
1 tbsp cream of tartar
1 tbsp vegetable oil
Food colouring (a few drops)
1 cup (75ml) water

Cook method:

- Pour the wet ingredients, including the food colouring, into a jug and mix to the desired colour.
- Put all the dry ingredients into a pan and then add the wet mixture, mixing it all together.
- Cook over a medium heat, stirring continuously until the mixture thickens and comes together into a dough.
- Turn out and knead for a few minutes until smooth.

Or you can use a no-cook method, which means that your child can be involved in all the steps! For this method, use all the ingredients as listed above, except for the water. This time use the same amount of *hot* water.

- Combine the dry ingredients together, and then mix in the oil.
- Add food colouring to the water until you have the desired colour.
- Add the coloured water, small amounts at a time, and mix well until a dough is formed.
- Turn out and knead for a few minutes until smooth.

Playdough will last for months if kept in an airtight container, zip-lock bag or tightly wrapped in cling film. You can try adding glitter to the mixture, or use a combination of food colours to discover what colours are created when colours are mixed (for example blue and yellow make green).

Saltdough

Ingredients:

1 cup (125g) flour
½ cup (25g) salt
½ cup (40ml) water (approximately)

Method:

- Mix the flour and salt together and slowly add the water a little at a time until you reach a dough consistency (you may not need all the water).
- Once mixed, turn out and knead for a few minutes until smooth (you may need to add a little more flour if it is sticking).

Saltdough will last for a few days if wrapped in cling film and kept in the fridge.

Alternatively, you can cook it: either in the oven on the lowest heat for 3 to 4 hours, or use a microwave in 10 to 15 second bursts until the dough is baked and dry. (Keep a close eye on the microwave method, as different microwaves have differing power levels). Once dry and cool, you can paint the models and/or use PVA glue to stick things on to decorate your design.